Uncovering Stories of Faith

by
Janet Ruffing

Paulist Press

New York Mahwah

Library of Congress Cataloging-in-Publication Data

Ruffing, Janet, 1945–
    Uncovering stories of faith : spiritual direction and narrative /
by Janet Ruffing.
      p. cm.
    Bibliography: p.
    ISBN 0-8091-3068-8
    1. Spiritual direction.   2. Discourse analysis, Narrative.
I. Title.
BX2350.7.R84 1989
253.5—dc19   89-3148
                                                CIP

Published by Paulist Press
997 Macarthur Boulevard
Mahwah, NJ 07430

Printed and bound in the
United States of America

Contents

Permissions

The material reprinted in *Uncovering Stories of Faith* first appeared in the following publications and is reprinted with permission: "My Story and 'The Story' " by Robert McAfee Brown, July 1975, p. 167, *Theology Today,* Princeton, N.J.; "Full of Life Now" by Barret J. Mandel, from *Autobiography: Essays Theoretical and Critical* edited by James Olney, pp. 68, 69, Princeton University Press, Princeton, N.J.; section from *Lifestory Conversations* by Dr. Roy Fairchild, pp. 14, 15, Presbyterian Church (U.S.A.), Louisville, Ky.; excerpt from *The Cloud of Unknowing, The Book of Privy Counseling* by William Johnston, pp. 182, 183, Doubleday, N.Y.; *Critical Inquiry* by R. Schafer, Vol. 7 (1980): 29–53, The University of Chicago Press; excerpts from *Truth and Method* by Hans-Georg Gadamer, p. 17, p. 211, p. 324, and *Christ: The Experience of Jesus as Lord* by Edward Schillebeeckx, p. 33, Crossroad, N.Y.; quote from *Human Experience* by Denis Edwards, Paulist Press, p. 27; material from *Classical Rhetoric and Its Secular Tradition from Ancient to Modern Times,* by George Kennedy, The University of North Carolina Press; "A Dwelling Place: Images and Our Experience of God" in *Studies in Formative Spirituality,* pp. 20, 21, Institute of Formative Studies; Semeia 13 from "The Narrative Function" by Paul Ricoeur, p. 182, Scholars Press; *Sacraments and Sacramentality* by Bernard Cooke, pp. 44, 45, Twenty-Third Publications; *On Knowing God* by Jerry H. Gill, pp. 70, 71, and *The Spiritual Exercises* by Gerald J. Campbell, The Westminster Press; *The Promise of Narrative Theology* by George W. Stroup, p. 111; *The Act of Reading: A Theory of Aesthetic Response* by Wolfgang Iser, pp. 34, 35,

Johns Hopkins University Press; *Spiritual Direction in the Desert Fathers* by Benedicta Ward, p. 66; *The Way; Stranger to Self-Hatred,* by Brendan Manning, p. 95, Dimension Books; "The Narrative Quality of Experience," *Journal of American Academy of Religion,* 39 (Sept. 1971) pp. 300, 301.

Acknowledgements

When this manuscript was near completion, I realized I had written about one small aspect of spiritual direction that could be explained and readily understood. At the same time, I continue to experience aspects of this ministry which remain mysterious, uncanny, and filled with awe—inexplicable occasions of grace.

I am, therefore, grateful for the gifts that have come to me through those who have served as my directors, Andrew Dufner, Helen Bunje, and Robert J. Egan, as well as for the men and women who entrusted themselves and their stories to me. Particular thanks to Sam and Mary for their generosity in sharing their lives with you through their cases and to the directors who granted me interviews.

Howard Gray gave me the initial clue to this approach to spiritual direction in a workshop he gave in Berkeley in 1978. He recommended that neophyte directors immerse themselves in fiction and drama in order to understand their directees. He may be surprised at this outcome from his remarks.

David Stagaman and Sandra M. Schneiders both improved the quality of this work in its conceptualization and expression through their careful attention to earlier drafts. What I learned from them about the process of writing and thinking has carried over to this final draft and into subsequent writing and mentoring of my students.

No project such as this is sustained without moral and financial support. I wish to thank the Sisters of Mercy, my family, and my friends who have supported and sustained me through two versions of this manuscript.

Fordham University generously provided support for the final manuscript preparation. I want to thank Micaela Mena Baker, whose friendship led to days of assistance with manuscript preparation, Catherine B. Nelson, who produced the final text, and my editor Douglas Fisher.

1

Introduction

> So abounding will that joy be that it will follow you to bed
> at night and rise with you in the morning. It will pursue
> you through the day in everything you do. . . . The joy
> and the desire will seem to be part of each other . . .
> though you will be at a loss to say just what it is that you
> long for. Your whole self will be transformed; your face
> will shine with an inner beauty; and for as long as you feel
> it, nothing will sadden you. A thousand miles would you
> run to speak with another who you knew really felt it and
> yet when you got there, find yourself speechless! And yet
> your only joy would be to speak of it . . . words fruitful,
> and filled with fire. . . .[1]

This quotation from a fourteenth century spiritual classic, *The Book of Privy Counselling,* expresses the ambivalence,
joy, and desire which often accompany the attempt to talk
about one's deepest experiences of God and their effects to
another who understands and welcomes them. It is this felt
need of individuals whose lives God has touched or who
themselves find there is "something more" in life they wish to
explore, seek, or welcome that leads people into a spiritual
direction relationship. Experiences of "transcendence" leave
one with more questions than they answer.[2] They challenge,
allure, and invite personal response to the approach of the

1

Mysterious Other who draws near to individuals in the concrete situation of their particular life stories.

The help that one person gives another in order to encourage that person's spiritual development has long been
called spiritual direction in the western Christian tradition,
and the term spiritual director is given to the person who
offers this help. Within this tradition, spiritual direction has
been a major element in the conception of the way people
grow in the spiritual life and has undergone considerable
change in its long history. Although the historical models of
spiritual direction vary, the practice of some form of direction
has remained constant. Currently, many people consider it to
be very important, with the consequence that an increasing
number of people are engaging in this process and a growing
body of literature about spiritual direction is emerging.[3]

Typological History of Spiritual Direction

A brief examination of six successive models of the spiritual direction relationship will situate historically the analysis
of the narrative aspects of the contemporary spiritual direction conversation.[4] These typological models are: the fourth
century desert *abbas/ammas,* the Benedictine monastic
model, the late medieval non-monastic model, the sixteenth
century Ignatian interventionist model, the seventeenth to
nineteenth century post-Tridentine director of conscience,
and the Vatican II contemporary model.

The Desert Abbas/Ammas
The desert tradition of spiritual direction emerged in the
fourth and fifth centuries in Egypt, Palestine, and Syria as a
model of spiritual guidance distinct from the ordinary pastoral care of Christians. Because of the isolation and harshness
of life in the wilderness and casualties among those who rashly

attempted the solitary search for God in the depths of their hearts, the need for guidance became extremely acute. Newcomers to the desert life began to seek out an elder, an *abba* or *amma* who had already been seasoned by solitude and so possessed an experiential knowledge of temptation and the life of prayer to guide them. The neophyte would either live with the elder or live nearby.

The title *abba/amma*—father/mother—indicated the preferred image of the relationship, child to parent, based in an experienced reality of spiritual paternity/maternity which characterized this wholly charismatic and freely chosen relationship.[5] This graced ability to facilitate the unfolding of the life of the Spirit in one's spiritual son or daughter depended on the dispositions of the seeker and the discerning "word" and life example of the elder. André Louf describes the dispositions needed in the seeker: "a sincere desire to know God's will and the beginning of detachment from all selfish desire."[6] These dispositions enabled the seeker to come to the *abba* or *amma* and ask for a "word" of life. This "word," unique to each seeker, exerted a sacramental effect. Its purpose was to reveal and heal the particular weaknesses or deficiencies in the seeker.[7] This word was more than information or instruction but a way toward God. As such, it "was not to be discussed or analyzed or disputed in any way; at times, it was not even understood; but it was to be memorized and absorbed into life."[8]

Further, this relationship of filiation to the spiritual parent implied docility, obedience, and trust. The seeker entrusted all interior movements of his or her heart to the elder for spiritual discernment. This manifestation of the heart was clearly distinct from sacramental confession, a rare practice in this period. The neophyte brought to the surface of awareness the abiding tendencies and dispositions of heart—how he or she was tempted and the dominant passions most capable of confusing or deceiving a person in the quest for God. This dialogue could include not only interior movements but precise details about daily life in the cell. Its purpose was to enhance spiritual freedom and eventually bring about the deep peace which results from depth of self-knowledge and a corresponding reliance on the grace of God. This relationship was lifelong, not severed even by the death of the elder. However, because the relationship was of a wholly charismatic[9] nature, it could be reversed if the neophyte eventually surpassed the spiritual maturity of the elder.[10]

The relationship with the elder was contextualized in a whole life style which recognized the importance of the role of the elder but which also took care to relativize it. In the desert God was always the first teacher. The cell was the second. And within the cell was the guidance of holy scripture.[11] Only then came the *abba/amma* as a help in discernment and a protection against self-deception, self-will, and other evasions which prevented the person from receiving the gift of God uniquely. The "words" spoken and the advice given in this form of direction were always particular, concrete, and intended exclusively for the person addressed. The teaching or instruction was wholly unsystematic and was valid only for someone in an analogous situation. This model was the most individualized form of spiritual direction in the tradition, since it preceded general or systematic accounts of spiritual development which affected the practice of spiritual direction in later periods. At this stage, it was completely distinct from the confessor/penitent model. It placed a high value on obedience and docility of the younger person in relationship to the *abba/amma*. The express purpose of this submission was to free the younger person from self-will in a life style that was highly individualistic. One became a guide to others only on the basis of personal experience and the gift of discernment combined with the willingness to release the other from guidance when its purpose had been achieved.

Medieval Models

THE BENEDICTINE MONASTIC MODEL

The Benedictine monastic model of spiritual direction incorporated many features of the desert tradition while it innovated in other respects.[12] Although Benedict maintained the ideal of the "spiritual father" rooted in the desert tradition as his primary model for the role of the abbot of a stable community, the context of this relationship was dramatically different. The monastery was a *schola,* a place of training; its purpose was to lead others to salvation through the practice of the ascetic life.

The Rule itself and the community which was its living expression became the primary form of guidance. The Rule carefully spelled out the external details of life as well as the desired internal dispositions of heart all were to practice, namely, obedience, silence, humility, and fraternal love. All, including the abbot, were obliged first of all to be obedient to the provisions of the Rule. The abbot was charged with the responsibility of guiding the monks according to individual needs and differences and was to be chosen for qualities of spiritual leadership, especially "discretion."[13] He was no longer a purely charismatic figure around whom others gathered, but an office-holder charged with an obligation to teach and direct his community. Although the Rule encouraged a form of individual guidance through manifestation of conscience to the abbot (RB 7.44), in practice his teaching was often directed to the community as a whole.

In addition to the abbot's serving many of the monks as a spiritual father, other experienced monks, the *seniores,* were

chosen freely by seasoned monks and appointed for newcomers (RB 58.6). The novice director was charged with passing on the whole of a way of life by means of personal example, reading and explaining the rule, and discerning the
candidates' suitability for the life. William of St. Thierry, an
early Cistercian, emphasized the role of the elder in relationship to a novice. The novice was to entrust himself totally to
his spiritual father "to be formed in God, in the feelings and
the spirit of humility" because he himself lacked discretion
and the ability to be discerning in his own case.[14] The role of a
"spiritual father" was not restricted to novices. The more
mature members were encouraged to a fraternal obedience to
a guide because

> . . . in such matters the eye of someone else often has a
> clearer view of us than our own. Someone else, someone
> whose will is not a prey to the same fervor, is often a better
> judge of our acts than we are. For often either through
> negligence or through self-love we have a mistaken idea of
> ourselves.[15]

In addition to this assistance with discernment, one also
sought in a spiritual father encouragement in the spiritual life
and a knowledge of God derived from the guide's personal
contemplative experience.[16]

In this model of spiritual direction, a trend toward institutionalizing the essential characteristics of the earlier model
appeared alongside the charismatic element. Individual care
for each, discernment, and receiving the manifestation of
heart from the directee continued. However, these functions
could be dispersed among an experienced monk, an appointed novice director, and/or the abbot. These people were
to be chosen on the basis of a recognized charism to perform
this role. An external rule of life and a stable community were

the milieu in which this direction relationship existed with the effect of relativizing the role of the guide. The relationship to the elder was originally distinct from the confessor/penitent relationship. However, the practice of sacramental confession gradually began to merge with the direction relationship. With the establishment of the practice of confession in the universal church, frequent "devotional" confession became common for people seeking holiness of life, linking spiritual direction to the confessional until the contemporary period.[17] Obedience to the Rule, to the abbot and to the spiritual director continued as a valued method of tempering self-will, all further affected by a communal life of fraternal charity.

A similar model of spiritual direction existed in women's monasteries. The abbess functioned as a spiritual director for her nuns as did other women in the community. During some parts of the Middle Ages, abbesses held jurisdiction over the male clerics who served the community in a liturgical capacity.[18] However, with the gradual practice of more frequent confession and increasing clericalism in the church, the women, abbesses included, were all to a certain extent eventually subject to the direction of male, cleric confessors.

MEDIEVAL NON-MONASTIC MODEL

Although the Benedictine/Cistercian monastic model of spiritual direction dominated the entire middle ages, new developments in lay piety began to emerge in the twelfth to fifteenth centuries. The Dominican Order (founded in 1216 by Dominic Guzman) was characterized by its concern "to be useful to the souls of our neighbors" and initiated a "third order" group for lay members.[19] The Franciscans (founded ca 1221 by Francis Bernadone) began as a mendicant lay group, espousing poverty of life and preaching the gospel. Simultaneously, in northern France, Flanders, and Holland, new forms of the *vita apostolica* emerged in the form of beguine communities.[20] The *vita apostolica* was characterized by two major features, poverty of life and preaching the gospel.

Vandenbroucke characterizes the non-clerical, non-monastic forms of spiritual direction resulting from these new forms of evangelical life as "extra-hierarchical and charismatic."[21] A number of holy women, *mulieres religiosae* (the name given to those women who were non-monastic in life style yet totally dedicated to God), were recognized spiritual directors. They were mystics and usually ecstatics.[22] Among these were Hadewijch of Antwerp (writings date ca 1220–1240), Catherine of Siena (1347–1380), Julian of Norwich (1343–1416), and Catherine of Genoa (1447–1510).

Hadewijch, leader of a beguine community, was responsible for the spiritual formation of her companions. Her letters, such as Letter 15.5, testify to her role as spiritual guide:

> . . . and closely observe, with regard either to myself or others in whom you seek sincere practice of virtue, who they are that help you to improve, and consider what their life is. For there are all too few on earth today in whom you can find true fidelity; for almost all people now want from God and men what pleases them and what they desire or lack.[23]

Hadewijch's career was a stormy one, as she was eventually rejected by her community. The letters were probably written both while she was still part of the community and after her separation from it.

As a recluse, Julian of Norwich was consulted as a person of good counsel. *The Book of Margery Kempe* is a contemporary witness which describes in considerable detail Margery's experience consulting Julian. Margery claims she was led to ask advice of Julian with regard to the special grace which God had accorded her, "for the ankres was expert in swech thyngys and good cownsel cowd geuyn." She reported Julian's balanced advice and described the consultation in glowing terms: "Much was the holy dalliance that the anchoress and this creature had by communing in the love of our Lord Jesus Christ on the many days they were together."[24] Although a visionary, Julian exhibited a markedly lesser degree of ecstatic phenomena than did the other women discussed below.

Catherine of Siena and Catherine of Genoa were both laywomen. Catherine of Siena became a member of the *Mantellate,* a Dominican tertiary group, and continued to live at home. Catherine of Genoa, although she wanted to become a nun at thirteen, agreed to a family arranged, political marriage. Unhappily married for ten years, she underwent a mystical conversion. Thereafter, she, with her husband's agreement, gave herself to the care of the sick, as a nurse and director at the Pannetone Hospital. Julian and the two Catherines all survived outbreaks of plague in their cities. The two Catherines were noted for their care of plague victims.

The two Catherines attracted groups of disciples which included all kinds of people, cleric and lay. These saintly women engaged in spiritual conversations with them, forming their spirituality and inspiring their active charity. Catherine of Siena called her followers her "family" of which she was their acknowledged "mamma" regardless of the age differences among them. She also dictated numerous letters of spiritual direction and was remarkable for her prophetic gift which allowed her to "read other people's secret thoughts and intentions."[25]

All four women wrote or dictated major spiritual writings which were the fruit of their mature mystical development and their experience with others.[26] They developed their own mystical theology out of their experience in concert with the tradition they had received. As spiritual directors, they were women, experienced in the spiritual life, who were sought out by others for instruction, encouragement in faith, and group and individual counsel. Hadewijch and the Catherines gave spiritual direction to the communities which gathered around them. All eloquently and profoundly communicated their spiritual teaching through their writing which was produced toward the end of their lives. Some extended their spiritual influence through their male disciples, a common model which included a number of other such women.[27]

Ignatian Interventionist Model

Ignatius of Loyola (1495–1556), through the development of *The Spiritual Exercises,* inaugurated a new model of spiritual direction, typified as interventionist. Ignatius developed the text of *The Spiritual Exercises,* a handbook for the one who gives the Exercises, based on experimental self-observation and experience in guiding others through this sequence of active, ascetical exercises.[28] These processes were designed to prepare and dispose "the soul to rid itself of all inordinate attachments, and, after their removal, of seeking and finding the will of God in the disposition of our life for the salvation of our soul."[29] Ignatius envisioned the director specifically as "one who gives the Exercises" usually in an enclosed setting of thirty days' duration (#20). He and his followers later amplified this text with additional commentary called *The Directory of the Exercises.*[30]

In this model, the director, having personal experience as an exercitant,[31] decides who is suitable to engage in this process (#18) and determines the manner of prayer and the subject of meditations, examinations of conscience, and imaginative contemplations (#4).[32] The director discerns the meaning, source, and directionality of the retreatant's affectivity, commonly referred to as "spirits," and gives instruction on the rules for discernment of spirits as the one making the Exercises requires (##7–11).[33] Finally, the director adapts the Exercises to each person (#4 and 18). In this active role, the director confronts the exercitant with processes and subject matter that arc designed to initiate a dynamic in the directee that is less likely to occur without this intervention. Its purpose is ordering the life and affections of the exercitant in such a way that the directee is disposed to encounter the creator directly and respond to God's initiative. After these interventions, the director assumes a background role in order to encourage the exercitant to derive personal meaning from the meditations and to savor this intimate contact with God.[34] Ignatius' image for this role is that of the balance point on a scale.

People who made the Exercises were to begin them with great generosity of heart and be willing to answer the director's questions about all relevant experiences. Without knowing the sins of the exercitant, the director is to be "kept faithfully informed about the various disturbances and thoughts caused by the action of different spirits" (#17).[35] Because the directee does not necessarily know the sequence or structure of the Exercises, the director needs to receive the retreatant's account of his or her experience in order to guide the person through the process.

This model of direction had an enormous impact on Counter-Reformation piety in the post-Tridentine Church. It was a form of direction adaptable to all pious people who had sufficient leisure to make the enclosed retreat. It was independent of monastic life style and had as its aim the formation of people who would be active in service to others. The proliferation of printed material, the spread of education through the college system, and an adaptation of this model of direction to the confessional were some of the reasons for its influence. In its founder's conception, this form of spiritual direction was highly individualized, a one-to-one relationship solely for the purposes of the Exercises.

However, by the seventeenth and eighteenth centuries the content of the Exercises had been adapted to group retreats, the formation of sodalities, and the preaching of missions. This model of direction became a common feature of confessional practice, no longer restricted to the special circumstances of the enclosed retreat.[36]

Post-Tridentine Director of Conscience

The model of spiritual director in the Catholic tradition after the Council of Trent (1545–1563)[37] emphasized the confessor/penitent relationship as the ordinary form of spiritual direction and dominated this tradition for three hundred years. According to the Tridentine definition of penance, the confessor/director assumed the role of judge and became a "quasi-superior" for penitents who were not under the authority of a religious superior.[38] In this model, obedience to the spiritual director became excessively valued. By the early twentieth century spiritual direction had come to be understood as the application of "principles and general rules to each person in particular."[39] One acquired these principles and rules through (a) the study of a systematic treatise on the spiritual life, (b) reading the great masters of the spiritual life, (usually from the sixteenth century to the present) and (c) the "practice of Christian and priestly virtues under the care of a wise director."[40] Although the need for personal experience in the spiritual life was acknowledged, spiritual direction was no longer presumed to be a charism. The link with sacramental confession resulted in spiritual direction becoming one of the functions of office and the responsibility of cleric-confessors.

In this context, spiritual direction became preoccupied with sin and "cases of conscience," implying the need for a specialist with appropriate theological and spiritual training who provided professional solutions for special cases and problems.[41] It is not surprising that scrupulosity emerged as a frequent spiritual problem and theme in this period. This model of direction tended to concern itself with decisions about specialized religious vocations and the directee's progress in mental prayer. Moreover, directors viewed themselves as guardians of orthodoxy and teachers of "safe" methods in the face of the threat posed by the Protestant Reformation and various mystical movements of the times, such as quietism, illuminism, and Jansenism. For these directors the avoidance of heresy and of dubious forms of mysticism was a major responsibility of their role.[42] In this model, spiritual direction had become institutionalized.

The theological context of this model of spiritual direction was an almost exclusively hierarchical view of the mediation of grace and God's will.[43] The relationship itself was clearly lacking mutuality. Non-mutual images for the relationship include: physician/patient, father/child, superior/subject, confessor/penitent, and, from Francis de Sales, guiding "angel, not merely a man."[44]

The terminology of spiritual direction, director, and directee derives from this historical period and continues to carry connotations of overbearing authority and infantalizing obedience. Although there were a number of very good and saintly spiritual directors who greatly helped holy people, during this time, the inherent authoritarianism of the model and the ideology that accompanied it frequently resulted in autocratic, incompetent, mediocre, and even ignorant directors exercising tyrannical control over the directee. As early as the sixteenth and seventeenth centuries, prominent voices spoke out against the harm that was being done to people by such directors. Among these critics were John of the Cross (1542–1591), Teresa of Avila (1515–1582), and Dom Augustine Baker (1575–1641).[45]

An excessive valuation of the role of spiritual direction in Christian life resulted in peculiar inversions in metaphorical descriptions of the relationship between God, the director, and the person seeking direction. For example, a book or a rule of life could take the place of spiritual direction.[46] And Thérèse of Lisieux wrote of Jesus as "the Director of directors."[47] Descriptions such as these reflect a persistent temptation for the director to forget that his role was purely mediational and to over-identify with being God's representative, assuming too much authority over the directee.

Through the institutionalizing of spiritual direction, it became available to all Christians regardless of their particular vocation if they were able to find a suitable director/confessor. Canon law required members of ecclesially established orders to present themselves to confessors on a weekly basis as well as to different confessors quarterly. Within such orders, many functions of spiritual direction were also performed by novice directors and superiors although matters of conscience were restricted to the confessional.

The dominant model of spiritual direction in this period was inherently clerical and sexist in its assumptions. The director applied abstract principles and rules to another's life. Although some of these principles were derived inductively from experience, conclusions were drawn deductively from the principles. The concrete experience of the person seeking direction had only relative value and was not necessarily taken into account in the formulation of the principles and rules. Further, throughout the literature, the extreme distrust of and devaluation of women led to common rules and admonitions to confessors that implied that women were untrustworthy, susceptible to illusions, and incapable of mature development in the spiritual life.[48] Women were consequently subject to ecclesiastical male authority to validate their religious experiences, approve their writings, and confirm their authenticity without their having access to the same theological education or training. Under these circumstances, in the delicate relationship of spiritual direction which requires self-disclosure and trust, women either entered into this process with men who were conditioned to be prejudiced against them or only superficially availed themselves of spiritual direction.

Contemporary Model

A contemporary model of spiritual direction, which is in marked contrast to the previous authoritarian, sacramental one, has evolved in the ecclesial and cultural context of the Second Vatican Council. The post-Tridentine model was particularly uncongenial to the Reformation churches and, within Roman Catholicism, restricted the scope and focus of spiritual direction. The contemporary model is largely once again charismatic and non-institutional. Spiritual direction has become distinct from the sacrament of penance as it was in some earlier models. People freely choose a spiritual director of either sex who may or may not share the same Christian life style. Directors are usually expected to be knowledgeable about the spiritual tradition, to understand the dynamics of spiritual development and prayer from personal experience, and to be able to assist with discernment. In this era of psychological self-consciousness, directors are also expected to be conversant with major psychological theories and concepts, especially developmental psychology.

Although there is a certain amount of asymmetry in the relationship, both persons prefer to view each other as mutually growing in the spiritual life and related to each other as brothers and sisters in Christ. One person assumes a reflecting/listening role in relation to the other only in the restricted situation of the spiritual direction conversation. Unlike the monastic model, in the contemporary model frequently directors and directees do not necessarily live with each other nor relate to one another outside the time of direction.

In canonically established religious orders and seminaries, spiritual direction is frequently distinguished from the formation goals of passing on a way of life within a particular community or judging a candidate's suitability for priesthood or a particular form of religious life. People institutionally charged with supervising the formation of new members generally do not also assume the role of spiritual director.

In the contemporary model, the importance of authority and obedience has changed. The belief that God speaks primarily and most reliably through persons in authority has been relativized through the complementary belief that people, in general, peers and subordinates as well as those in authority, mediate God's will and grace to an individual. What is required is the ability to discern God's presence and activity through various possible mediations. A profound respect for freedom of conscience and the responsibility of the directee for personal choices pervades contemporary spiritual direction. Directors, conscious of the psychological dynamic of transference, usually refuse a directee's inclination to hand over decision-making or authority in an attempt to avoid personal responsibility. Obedience is perceived to be a virtue when a person is attempting to listen to and recognize God's claim in a concrete situation. The director holds authority primarily by virtue of the assertion of the truth of a situation or by virtue of actual superior knowledge. The focus shifts from valuing obedience for its own sake without reference to the merits of that which is commanded to the development of discerning hearts. Thus, discernment in relationship to the concrete situations which confront a person becomes central.

The role of the director is usually imaged as genuinely helpful yet auxiliary. Spiritual directors describe themselves as co-discerners, listeners, companions, midwives, soul-friends, and co-travelers. God, or the Holy Spirit, is the acknowledged guide or director for each person, and the human spiritual director's role is to help the other recognize and respond to the divine leading.[49]

Instead of applying principles or rules to individual cases, the contemporary model of spiritual direction concerns itself with the concrete, religious experience of the individual. Influenced by a theology of the human person which takes embodiment, historicity, social context, and process seriously, and a theory of knowledge which moves from the concrete and particular to the general and abstract, contemporary spiritual directors value the particular and unique experiences of their directees in a quite different way than did those in previous periods.

The Problem of Terminology

The classical terminology for spiritual direction is not altogether satisfactory. Spiritual paternity/maternity is insufficiently egalitarian for many directors and directees and seems to apply to a rather limited number of actual spiritual direction relationships. Some people prefer to use a friendship model for spiritual direction. Although a fully mutual spiritual friendship may occur for some people, this seems not to be the case for the majority. Furthermore, gifted spiritual directors who are sought out by a number of people cannot possibly enter into each relationship in a fully mutual way. Despite its appeal, the language of spiritual friendship neither differentiates the roles in spiritual direction nor accounts for the asymmetry that usually exists.

Many people have a distinct aversion both to the clerical model of confessor/penitent and to the medical-psychiatric models of therapist/client or doctor/patient as helpful ways of describing the direction relationship. Likewise, many find the authoritarian overtones of director/directee language repugnant. Nevertheless, many people do continue to use director/

directee terminology because it distinguishes the respective roles in the relationship, it allows one to relate the contemporary experience to the tradition, and it is possible to redefine the terms acceptably.[50] Although this terminology is not without disadvantages, I use it because of its link to the tradition and for the sake of clarity in distinguishing roles.

Assumptions about Spiritual Direction

Although the aim of spiritual direction has remained constant, namely, growth in the spiritual life of the person seeking direction, our conception of it has changed throughout history. For the purpose of this study which deals with one aspect of the spiritual direction conversation, its actual narrativity, I make the following assumptions about spiritual direction: 1. The purpose is the spiritual growth of the person seeking direction. 2. Two Christians are interpersonally engaged with one another in an ongoing relationship for this purpose. 3. The focus of the conversations is the experienced interaction of God with the person seeking direction and that person's response to these movements both within prayer and in daily life. 4. Both persons participate in discernment, in discriminating how God seems to be leading the person toward action or response. 5. Although both persons are fallible Christians trying to follow the leading of God in their lives within the context of Christian faith and community, there is a presupposition that the person who serves as guide or director has some capacity to be helpful to the other by virtue of the depth of personal graced experience, the gift of discernment, experience with self and others, and sufficient knowledge of the spiritual tradition and ordinary human development. 6. Because the focus of direction is on spiritual growth, the spiritual direction encounter presupposes that the person seeking direction is consciously relating to God, however mysteriously or vaguely named. 7. This experienced relationship to a transcendent other or its possibility places the conversation within the sphere of divine influence for both persons. God is the one who leads, directs, guides.[51]

Narrative in Spiritual Direction

There are various ways one could analyze the transaction that is going on in spiritual direction. I would like to suggest a way which has not been explored before, namely, to identify that which is put forth by the directee as a narrative and to analyze the transaction in categories appropriate to narrative.[52] My attention to the narrativity of spiritual direction emerged only gradually in my experience of spiritual direction as both a directee and a director. I chose a narrative lens for examining this experience because, whatever else also happens, there is a fundamental narrativity present to some degree in spiritual direction. Except for the rather rare instances when gifted spiritual directors read people's hearts without their verbal self-disclosure, what most directors have to work with is the verbal and non-verbal discourse of the person seeking direction. Frequently, and in my experience characteristically, what the directee offers is a narrative. Insofar as one is trying to understand and respond to what another says, one is engaged as well in a hermeneutical process—understanding and interpreting. Consequently, I propose to construct a theoretical framework which explains why people produce narratives in the contemporary context of spiritual direction, account for the effects this narrative activity has on the people involved, identify and describe the distinctive features of these narratives and elaborate some of the implications of this narrative analysis for the practice of spiritual direction.

My analysis is primarily a theoretical approach constructed from a variety of sources. However, it is also based on my extensive experience in spiritual direction as both a director and a directee. As a directee, I became more aware of the features of my own story through the telling of it. I also wondered why I told my own story differently to different directors and noticed that at a certain point in my development I began to tell a different story about myself. I take my experience to be typical of at least some others and draw from it occasionally. A series of case studies of experiences of spiritual direction provides a common basis for reflection throughout the discussion. These cases, in fact, turn out to be stories of direction, secondary narratives constructed from memory about the primary narrative that was unfolding in spiritual direction. There are short verbatim sections which, I hope, will give the reader unfamiliar with this process a sense of the way the story gets told in the actual situation. These cases are all written by directees from their point of view. The case studies follow as examples of contemporary spiritual direction and provide a concrete, shared reference point for the subsequent theoretical discussion.

2

Case Histories of Spiritual Direction:
Sam and Mary

Both of these case studies were written by the directees expressly for inclusion in this work. Both reconstructed their narratives from memory some time after the events. Sam wrote his narrative during the fall following the year's experience in spiritual direction recorded in his case. Mary wrote hers three years after the retreat she describes. Both cases are written entirely from the directees' points of view.

This method of producing a case history respects the narrators' control over self-disclosure and honors their storied interpretations of their experiences. This procedure is in direct contrast to case histories written from the director's point of view which, of course, is a different story. Sam knew about my interest in narrative in spiritual direction but had not read my theoretical construction prior to composing his narrative. Mary, on the other hand, had read Chapter Five of the original dissertation. That fact did not seem to affect her narrative appreciably although, as a director, she tended to respond naturally to narrative elements in her directee's stories.

In order to protect the writers' identities, pseudonyms are used for them and others mentioned in their case studies. Sam is one of many people I have seen for spiritual direction while Mary recounts a retreat experience with another very competent director. In Mary's case, the director gave more conscious attention to the emotional issues Mary was experiencing rather than responding explicitly to the rich texture of narrative details embedded in her story. Consequently, the reader may be able to sense the contrast between a narrative approach to spiritual direction and a more psychological approach. After writing her case history, Mary agreed to an interview in which I explored with her some narrative responses to her story. Some of that material will be referred to along with the discussion and analysis of both of these cases.

Sam's Experience of Spiritual Direction

Sam is a member of the Society of Jesus, a religious order of men usually known as Jesuits. He was nearing the end of formation and ministerial training leading to ordination to the priesthood and was in year eleven of membership in the Society, having completed novitiate, philosophy, and regency, all stages in Jesuit formation. He was in the second year of a three year Master of Divinity degree program and was living in a small group with several other members of the order. This group related to the larger community of Jesuits working or studying in the academic community and was affected by decisions made by the rector and his staff as well as being accountable to them.

I asked Sam to write his story because my experience of him in direction very clearly supported my thesis. Since he was simultaneously engaged in psychotherapy, there was less psychological counseling and more spiritual direction in his situation than is frequently the case with others. Additionally, because he was learning to tell a Freudian story in order to reinterpret his childhood experiences, Sam was able to see and experience clearly how his experience in spiritual direction resulted in a different story from the one he was constructing in therapy. The differences seemed not so much to be opposing interpretations of experience, but rather telling portions of the story of therapy and other experiences within the context of faith.

Sam's Story

I am a thirty year old member of a religious community; I am currently studying theology and will be ordained to presbyteral ministry in June. During my time in religious life, I have had ongoing spiritual direction of varying quality. My previous director was transferred from Berkeley, and a year ago I began work with my present director. We had been in one class together, and she had done some work with my previous director, so she was not a total stranger to me. I chose to work with her because of good, personal impressions; as I thought about working with her, the idea of working with a woman grew more appealing. I had never done spiritual direction with a woman before, and as I was planning to begin psychotherapy with a man, I thought the balance of male and female input would be helpful.

The academic year that this case study covers was one of intense personal and spiritual deepening. The previous year had been a very difficult one due to a confluence of a number of personal issues. As I began my work with this director, I was aware of a need for healing, for integration of those personal issues, and for some sort of decision regarding my application for ordained ministry. Soon after beginning, I began an ongoing psychotherapy process; then and now, I felt the processes to be related, but dealing with different issues in my personal identity. Spiritual direction consisted of meetings every other week for approximately one and one-half hours. During that time, our conversations covered a number of topics.

This case study presents the year in such a way as to give the reader a sense of the period's ongoing dynamic. Within that narrative, I will focus on three overlapping topics: prayer and religious experience, discernment, and, for lack of a better word, "moments of insight."

I have a clear memory of our first meeting in early September. My way of presentation in a significant interview is to throw "bait on the waters," so to speak. I begin very generally, filling out nothing of the story. I get a sense of how the person is going to respond, and if that sense is positive, he/she has my trust. I tend to be honest and revelatory rather quickly once I trust the other. I was true to form in that meeting. After some small talk, I gave a very brief and vague sketch of my life, leaving out significant details. She listened, and then said, "Would you like to tell me a little more about those issues?" I remember very quickly that I was not threatened by the question. I intuitively sensed that the director was trustworthy, and decided to tell much of my story then and there—a disastrous and difficult previous year, my struggles in coming to grips with some aspects of my identity, my decision to seek psychotherapy, my moving to a new community, the problems in my family. I surprise myself with my honesty in such initial situations, and I think my director was somewhat surprised in this one.

The conversation moved to prayer, which I described, in a somewhat embarrassed way, as not well focused, having consistency but little else. She then encouraged me to describe my praying—what I actually did in prayer. I used the phrase "yakking with God," walking in the neighborhood and talking familiarly with the Lord. The director affirmed my way of prayer; she used the phrase "yakking with God" positively, and while encouraging me "to be quiet once in a while so that it's a conversation, not a monologue," affirmed my style of prayer. No one had ever done that for me. I was appreciative and told her so. We talked a little then about introverted and extraverted prayer—mine is clearly the latter—the validity of different styles, and the possibility of "being silent in movement." This was wonderful for me; I confessed that I had never found yoga postures helpful. All of this was the first conversation about my prayer style that I had ever had. It was a breakthrough experience for me, which cemented my trust of the director.

As can be seen, my understanding of prayer was rather limited and limiting. I also tended to ignore God experience that did not fit those limits and to downgrade experiences that I could explain away or psychologize. One such experience occurred early in October.

S: I want to tell you about something that happened. I really lost it.

J: Tell me what happened.

S: Well, I was at the diaconate ordination, and I usually get weepy-eyed at those things to begin with. But once the rite of ordination started, I lost it. I just started crying, especially as the names of people I knew well were called. I cried for about twenty minutes—in fact, R., who was sitting next to me, held my head to his chest, I was crying so hard. And I couldn't stop, and people were looking at me . . .

J: What did you feel as this was happening?

S: I felt an overwhelming acceptance by God. In spite of my own doubts about ordination and all, I had the feeling that I was accepted just the way I am—that if there are any problems, they are mine, not God's.

J: Do you realize what happens when you describe that experience as "losing it" . . . that you are giving priority to the embarrassment rather than the presence of God? I don't think you lost it. God touched you in a very powerful and personal way.

I understood her point, and that helped to transform the experience into a touchstone of God's presence over the year.

I am a slow learner, though. About a month later, I was sheepishly describing an experience of tears and God's presence I had while listening to a contemporary song ("I Need You" by the Pointer Sisters). I remember introducing it by saying, ". . . this is kind of corny . . ."

> J: Experience of God is not "corny." By describing it that way, you are downgrading the power of the experience. Let the experience be what it is.
> S: I understand what you are saying.

My tendency to slight my experience of God has at least part of its source in a fear of getting too involved with God. I suspect I am afraid of what might happen if I take it all at face value. Another event of tying my relationship closer to God occurred in March. At that time I was experiencing great sadness and pain regarding my family.

> J: As you are talking, I can't help but think of Jesus' agony in the garden. What you are describing is your own experience of that. Perhaps you can let that become part of your prayer . . . to let the Lord give you a way to express what you don't have words for.
> S: You know, I've been thinking about that scene for some reason, but I'd never made the connection . . .

I did make the connection, and it has given me a lasting insight on how to incorporate the Jesus story into my own.

In addition to focusing on experiences of God, our spiritual direction conversations frequently dealt with experiences of living in a small Jesuit community and relationships with individuals. Autumn was a good time for me. Academically, I was in a challenging semester that was going well. My new community was turning out wonderfully. We were a group of eight, many of whom were on the rebound from difficult experiences the previous year, and we meshed well. As a community we chose to deal with a member of our house whose alcohol consumption was a concern to us. This was a confrontational situation in which I played a strongly supportive role. I found myself amazed that a community could respond to conflict positively and was equally amazed that people respected what I said. In direction, we discussed the dynamics of all of this, especially regarding the process of the alcohol intervention. As the son of a deceased, alcoholic father, I was particularly sensitive to and affected by a person showing signs of alcoholic behavior. Direction helped me clarify my own needs and expectations in this situation. Eventually, my relationship with this man became very rewarding.

Two relationships became important. One was with someone I had lived with the previous year and with whom I had not gotten along. Much healing was brought to that relationship. The other is a relationship that continues to be significant for me. In October I began going out to lunch once a month with another member of my living group. This relationship has become a solid friendship.

In addition to beginning a new spiritual direction relationship, I initiated therapy in a classical psychoanalytic mode. This experience was both difficult and rewarding. As I described above, I tend to reveal myself full-force when comfortable. Consequently, therapy moved through issues with rapidity. As the therapeutic relationship became a regular one, my focus in spiritual direction moved to another dominant issue—ordination.

Over the year, I suppose there were a number of small discernments, but I think they were all related to my decision to apply for ordination to the priesthood. My letter of petition needed to be written by the end of January. The topic was part of the direction conversation from October on, and it took center stage between Thanksgiving and the middle of January. I had m⸱ ⸱ᵥ issues around it. The first to deal with was my freedom to apply, which demanded also the freedom not to apply. We dealt with this soon after I spent an evening with my mother in the middle of October.

> S: I feel as though she's got it all planned out . . . she's really looking forward to it . . . and I understand it . . .
> J: But you don't have the freedom to say no . . .
> S: I can say no if I want, but I don't know what I want yet.
> J: Maybe to tell your mother that you don't know will give you the space you need in which to decide.

As a matter of fact, it did. Telling my mother took the pressure off the decision, and allowed me to deal with the next issue: readiness. I felt that I was not ready to be ordained. I had not really clarified this when I spoke about it in direction. I remember saying that I didn't have my act together yet. We explored some causes of that feeling—being in therapy, moving communities, etc. Going through them, I realized that they weren't the issue. The key was to realize, as I did in direction, that I would never be "ready," that God uses me as I am for ministry. It is God doing the work, not my "act" that is or isn't together.

From readiness arose feelings of unworthiness. In one session, I told how I had this vague feeling of not being good enough.

> J: If it's OK with you, I'd like you to try and visualize this feeling.
> S: I'm game.
> J: Close your eyes . . . relax . . . let yourself picture this force . . . when you can, describe it to me.

S: (some silence) It's a man, or boy, smaller than me . . .
it's wooden . . . just standing there, trying to scare me
with a roar, but he's just a small puppet . . . it's Pinoc-
chio! (laughter)

J: (with somewhat of a mocking scowl) . . . not so powerful after all.

I remember feeling foolish, but also sure that worthiness
was not the issue. That revealed itself in the conversation
following.

J: What else are you uneasy about in all this?

S: Well, all of my work in therapy is making me wonder
about my attitudes toward family life.

J: Tell me a bit more about this.

S: I knew I had a problem with my Dad because of his
drinking and erratic behavior at home. But now, I'm
getting in touch with very painful feelings about my
Mom. Our family life was really pretty difficult, you
know.

J: Is it possible that you chose Jesuit life partly because
your experience of family life was so conflictual and
confusing?

S: That's it. I'm wondering if moving toward ordination is
running away from marriage and family life.

J: Would you be willing to take this issue to prayer and
see what happens? Try to imagine what kind of marriage and family life you might have if you weren't a
religious. As you try to imagine that, recall what you
contribute to your local community. See if you can
imagine something different from your experience at
home and ask God what he wants for you.

S: I think I could do that.

That prayer encounter was pretty powerful. I found I
could imagine a healthy and harmonious family scene, com-

plete with a garden to work in and a job teaching high school.
I even felt confident about being emotionally sensitive to a
wife and children. But when I brought all that to prayer, I felt
even more strongly attracted to priesthood and Jesuit life. I
prayed over all this and made a decision that had some
freedom.

The scene shifts to early February.

S: Well, I wrote it.
J: Congratulations! Tell me about it.
S: I sat down where I pray and began to write. And I cried
    . . . I felt confirmed . . . and the letter just flowed. I
    made very few changes for the final draft.
J: Sounds as if the Spirit has been moving with you
    through the whole process.

The year continued well. Community continued to be
wonderful, and I found myself growing rooted in the new
house with the people there. I experienced a personality conflict with one member of the community which direction
helped me clarify. Therapeutically, ongoing day-to-day material was present, but my main agenda was working out my
relationship with my father, one which was far more complex
and in which I had had far more power than I realized. Obviously, such insights helped me in day-to-day living as well,
but my focus in therapy was on the past. The work was always
difficult, and very difficult at times. As I went through therapy, the question of ordination was present. At no time did
any issues which would have suggested a delay in moving
toward ordination present themselves. I felt grounded in that
decision even as my whole life was periodically up for reinterpretation.

Into the spring, community issues dominated direction.

There was a serious question as to where our community would be living the next year, and direction helped me to separate my personal authority issues from those involving community politics. My director's experience as a woman religious who has been through her battles was very helpful here. Through talking about the personal and political aspects of decision-making about community housing, I got to the point where I could lay this issue aside and not take the whole thing personally.

Lest it seem that only critical conversations occurred in spiritual direction, it is important to say that our sessions also had their non-critical moments, and I think our conversation helped me to gain insight on those as well. Two incidents stand out for me, one in the fall and one in the spring. The earlier one centered around the aforementioned evening with my mother, in which she related some family history that was both convoluted and inappropriate. As I grappled with that, my director suggested I look at my mother's experience as a Catholic woman, married in the early 1950's to an alcoholic man who died and left her a widow.

> J: Do you realize that she couldn't talk about the things she told you? She was expected to be quiet and raise a family. What she's talking about are things she couldn't talk about then.
> S: But why me? And why over dinner?
> J: Because somehow, you're safe. She may not realize what she's saying, but she's saying it.

This insight continues to be tremendously helpful as I deal with her. Another type of insight occurred in the spring, again around the extreme sadness and pain I was experiencing regarding my family.

S: I feel as though this pain is like an open, running sore, one that just has to ooze and bleed until it dries, and when it heals, it will leave this big scar.

J: Does it have to leave a scar?

S: Huh?

J: Well, can't healing take place without leaving a scar? Can a wound heal cleanly, leaving only a trace of a scar, or no scar at all?

S: I guess it could. I never thought of that.

J: The way you think about it will shape the way you heal.

The wound has almost healed, and I don't think the scar will be huge.

As the school year ended, I found myself pleased with the results. Therapy continued to be difficult and profitable. My focus had shifted to my relationship with my mother, and direction was helpful here. The community stayed virtually intact and in the same place, both of which were a relief. My own self-image had shifted as well; I was better able to hear positive comments to me and about me. On a faith-sharing weekend late in April, one of my community members told me that I was one of the most impressive people he had ever lived with. I shared this experience with my director, all the while fumbling as to why it was so significant.

J: What strikes me is the fact that X, who gave you the compliment, is the one with whom you risked involvement in the alcohol intervention in the fall. In a way, you helped him do something about his drinking, something you couldn't do for your father. Do you see a link there?

I did, and I continue to see many of the links between the conversation of direction and my ongoing story. I hope the reader has caught the flavor of my experience of direction over the year. I see our conversations as allowing me to retell and reshape my own story, to clarify its meaning, and to give me better insight into its more significant events.

Mary's Experience of Retreat Direction

Mary is a young laywoman who is a participant in a degree program to prepare her for a ministry in retreat work, spiritual direction and teaching. In her narrative she offers an account of her experience of an important retreat. She tells about both her experience of prayer and her experience of retreat direction. Her recollection of the interviews during the retreat focused primarily on her director's accurate perception of the situational distress occasioned by her recent divorce and her emotional responses to it. As is often the case in spiritual direction, it is both appropriate and necessary to address these issues.

As I reflected with Mary, long after this retreat, we both felt that responses to the specific images which emerged in her narrative would have supported her needed growth better than suggesting new images or projecting a line of development in her relationship with God which was not yet in Mary's awareness. From this narrative, it is often difficult to know whether or not Mary told her director about a given experience in prayer when she also brings up another topic she needed to discuss. Consequently, when I use this case material for subsequent reflection, I can only base my commentary on what I know from Mary. Her director may well have been responding to a different version of Mary's experiences as well as having heard more of her story from her previous retreats. Consequently, I have no intention of critiquing another spiritual director's work from this partial perspective. Rather I hope to suggest an expanded repertoire of possible responses which might have followed from Mary's own narrative self-presentation.

Mary's Story

This case is the story of an eight day directed retreat which occurred three years ago when I was twenty-eight years old, two months after my husband left the marriage. I had been happily married for eight years when my husband, after completing an advanced degree, left suddenly by having an affair. This created a crisis for me. I was terrified, experiencing an immense sense of failure and loss. I couldn't believe that this could happen to me. Divorce was something that happened to other people who didn't care about their marriages and hadn't put time into them. In total shock I went on retreat. This was the third directed retreat I had had with the same spiritual companion with whom I had built up a relationship of trust. This trust was crucial at a time when the man I trusted most had betrayed me.

Arrival

I arrived at the retreat center feeling numb, yet pleased to be in that place of peace again. My spiritual companion came to meet me, gave me an all encompassing hug and said, "Mary, I was shocked to hear your news, I couldn't believe the words in your letter." My eyes just filled with tears. I didn't say anything. He added, "I want you to know, if you need more time to talk, if something comes up at an unscheduled time, just come and find me. I want this time to be as helpful as possible for you." It was life-giving to be so warmly accepted.

Day One

I just spent time settling in, sleeping and awakening my numb senses to the smells, tastes, and beauty that was surrounding me. I began to slow down, walk slower and become quieter externally and internally. I explored the sense of touch, absorbing and being saturated with the nature that surrounded me. The garden was beautifully cared for, with colorful, dainty flowers; the grassy areas were wide and inviting while in the distance the mountains reminded that there were peaks and valleys to climb during my retreat. I contrasted the stone of the buildings with the softness of the grass—all symbolically representing the many and varied emotions I would have at this time. The scripture passage I used that day was "as certain as the dawn he will come." I became certain of God's presence in the whole history of my relationship with him. I longed for that relationship to be more fulfilled.

Day Two

As I came to quiet before the Lord my openness and receptivity improved. I became more able to hear the Lord's words to me. I was quite aware of how lost, empty and rejected I felt but stopped intellectualizing about it and moved into the feelings. A friend had placed a copy of the prayer "Footprints" under my door. I used this as a constant reminder that God was with me.

I expressed to my spiritual companion that I felt I had lost my best friend, my confidant and my lover, and that all I had left was a profound sense of emptiness. I had an image of myself gradually disintegrating into nothing, by dissolving into a thousand tiny pieces that could never be repaired because they were so fragmented and brutally torn. I felt worthless and motionless with no chance of building a new future, no hope that I could ever be happy again. I felt that I had been tried, convicted and crucified publicly in a most demeaning and humiliating way. I felt like the Christ figure in a paraliturgy I'd done with my class before the retreat. We made

Christ a clown with a white face. As he was crucified someone came and tore his mask into a thousand tiny pieces. I identified with Christ's pain so much. My spiritual companion just listened and cared during all of this. He suggested that these feelings were natural, and that I was actually managing very well. We began to talk about B.

> R: Mary, who married whom? Did B. marry you or did you just want him to marry you?
> M: (after a shocked pause,) Yes, I married B.; he didn't marry me.
> R: One person cannot make a marriage no matter how hard he or she tries. You did the best you could.

This really helped me to begin to deal with the extreme sense of failure I was feeling. My spiritual director added, "Perhaps we may be able to see a glimmer of resurrection during the retreat."

I also talked about the nightmares I had been having, in which I would wake up paralyzed. I was afraid at home in the house. My spiritual companion's response was, "Do you think you could open just one window a little when you go home? It sounds as if you are shutting everyone out of your life."

I was so hurt I was unable to express it to anyone. I would often cry and cry on my own. The only event in Christ's life that could bear the weight of how I felt was the crucifixion. Prayer that day began in tears, darkness, silence. Then the image of Christ crucified began to take on much the same expression and scars my shattered face had. I came to know that my pain was his pain and his pain mine. Scars that were bleeding on his face were also bleeding on mine, yet his eyes revealed a great capacity for love and constant hope. In his torn, weeping and rejected state he embraced me. I became still and dwelt waiting, for I felt I had nothing else. I began to abandon my own being and really trust in God.

˙ EVENING

The thing I feared most, that I simply didn't want to talk about, was my sexuality; I knew that I had to face this.

M: R., what I really need to talk about is my sexuality. I am having a great deal of difficulty expressing in words what I want to say. I keep having a vision of B. making love with Y. This breaks my heart. He didn't tell me that this had happened but I knew. I dreamed about it, and when he was home the next morning I confronted him with this. I went to him to hug him and say it would be all right but he pushed me away. I kept remembering this rejection and longed for someone to hug me, to touch me and not to see me as repulsive.

R: Mary, that is a language that you are used to using; it is natural to want to keep using it. That is your language and it is beautiful. I have often found that people whose spouses have died experience similar feelings. They have found it extremely helpful to take these feelings of desertion, emptiness and longings to prayer. As your body aches for someone to touch you, allow the Lord to do this.

I thought very carefully about this and began to put it into action. I continually used the image of crucifixion. I knew that Jesus was with me. I felt I knew exactly what he felt like, torn, bleeding and broken in body, but his spirit was strong. His spirit became united with mine. This became life-giving and energizing. I began to feel more peaceful. I took a long walk that day. I ventured out into the countryside for about four miles. I climbed boulders of limestone and found a place where I could look down on a valley of ferns and undergrowth. Earlier I had stayed close to the retreat house. I had gone down into the caves where I'd be covered with over-hanging branches. At this point in the retreat, I felt I could look down on the world and get a wider vision. The sun was shining and I felt that I would try to hand over my feelings to God.

Day Three

This day we talked about how things were financially and how I would manage. I had many bills to pay and was very short of money. I hated having to take on this responsibility but reluctantly had worked out how I could gradually pay off all the bills.

> R: You are a very capable person, could be a leader, but you evade responsibility. You need to develop this now.

I was shocked to hear this. I talked about all the things B. did for me and how difficult I found it now that I had to do everything for myself.

> R: That was not good for you to discuss everything with B. and then let him make all the decisions. Why haven't you developed the parts of your personality that are like your father?

This really made me stop and think. I had had a difficult relationship with my father and abhorred his aggression. I, in response, had become particularly passive, timid, and non-as-sertive. I became determined to work on this.

> R: Are you angry about what B. did to you?
> M: No, I just love him so much I could never be angry.

R: You have a right to be. He let you down, shattered your hopes and dreams, and you're not angry?
M: Well, I'm not. (I had an inability to express my anger.)
R: If you get a chance, tell him how you feel.
M: Do you think I should? I thought it better to keep to myself.
R: No, be assertive about your feelings.

I did a profile of myself that day of the things God liked in me and the things I thought he disliked. I began to see myself as I really was. I became very upset about my sinfulness, yet at the same time knew that God only wished for me conversion. I experienced how understanding, tolerant, loving and positive the Lord was and how patient. That evening at the communal reconciliation I was asked to embrace my friend "Judas," the betrayer of my life. I struggled to name and embrace this all day and was finally happy to hand it over to the Lord that evening. I did this with an undertone of sadness that I could not love as I was loved. After this reconciliation I had an incredible sense of being healed.

Day Four

I felt that I was really opening myself to the Lord and was longing just to be filled with the Lord. I continued to take my feelings of loneliness and longing to prayer. I talked about my opportunity to grieve the loss of B. My spiritual companion suggested that I continue to pray the way I had been but to put more effort into structuring prayer time.

That evening I was restless, trying to pray. I couldn't and was annoyed with myself. I decided to take a walk through the garden. The stars were out. It was a beautiful clear autumn evening. Then I had an exchange of love that took me beyond control. I felt as if I were in a mystical garden, fresh and life-giving. I was alone and yet was not alone. I felt surrounded in light and felt weightless. There was an incredible sense of peace. I knew then that there was ultimately only myself and God. At first I felt frightened, but this was very quickly followed by a sense of confidence and freedom. This was all part of the mystery that began to heal me. The insurmountable problems facing me now took on new dimensions; they were still there, but were clothed with new meaning. Eventually I knew that I would have the energy to face them one by one. I came to know that I was loved unconditionally in a way I had not thought possible.

> R: How was your day?
> M: I am praying much better now.
> R: Can you describe your prayer to me?
> M: It's very difficult to put into words.
> R: Without saying too much to take away from the preciousness of the experience, could you just say something?

I described the experience of God in the garden. My spiritual companion looked pleased—reverent.

> R: I don't know what you did yesterday but whatever it was God is confirming your life. Just keep going the way you are with prayer.

Day Five

I had a dream that night that I found particularly significant to all that was happening. A young, shallow girl with a flawless face had been replaced by a scarred, wrinkled woman. The older woman had true beauty; her eyes were sad yet comforting and loving because I could see that she had suffered deeply and during this time had learned what loving really meant. It was then that I realized that if I really loved my husband, I would let him be free, and I would make a new life for myself, a life that would be richer and fuller than it had been previously. In direction, we talked about the possibility that since my self-image was changing, perhaps my image of God would need to change, too. R. suggested that I might like to use more maternal images of God such as those in Isaiah.

This appealed to me as I had been asking myself the crucial question: Would God desert me just as B. had? During this retreat God didn't leave me but became ever present, all-loving and totally understanding. I felt I was being penetrated by God. At the same time I was tentative. I had a reverence tinged with wonder and fear, yet I was confident that eventually things would come clear to me.

Day Six

I felt that I was being strengthened to go home and to live more confidently. I knew that God would be with me on that journey. That night I had a dream of the house being torn apart. I knew that B. was taking half the furniture while I was away. Although we had split it fairly, I was worried about what would be gone and how I'd manage. I also had to go back to school and face everyone again.

> M: I don't know what I am going to do with my life now. Do you think this is God's way of telling me I should join a religious order?
> R: (laughed) I don't think that would be a good idea.
> M: What could I do now? With no one to love, what would I do?

He advised me not to make any decisions while I was in a state of desolation.

Day Seven

During our final interview, my spiritual companion talked about the story of Thomas.

> R: Think of Thomas. Remember when he asked to put his hands into the wounds of Jesus. That unless he could do this he could not believe. Remember this as you go home. Thomas was so wise. He knew that in order for Christ to be authentic he needed to have suffered. In order for Thomas to mirror his master, to believe in a way that made their lives one, he too must become part of that suffering to enter it and to experience it.
>
> M: I had another dream which seems important. I was in an accident in which my head had come off. When I looked closely, there was still a tiny piece of skin attached. A friend put my head back on and was bandaging me.
>
> R: This is a sign that resurrection has begun. Your head wasn't quite off and the bandages were on.

I identified with Thomas later. This was a great comfort for me in my suffering. I felt I was being refined to become more like Christ. As I went home, I was scared yet hopeful. I felt my emptiness had been filled with the Lord, that I lived not alone but that Christ was in me. I was sober about what I had to face. I lived out of the retreat experience. Six months later it was still real, and I wrote my annulment papers with help from the retreat.

Conclusion

The retreat initiated the process of gradually reassembling the pieces of my story into a new, creative and exciting one. I found hope and knew that I wanted to be a lover of life again but a passionate lover. I was no longer someone's wife but an individual. I grew to know myself at my worst and had many of my fears and weaknesses identified. I felt that my spiritual companion had helped mediate God's wish that I be whole again. I began to try to build on my strengths and embrace my weaknesses. I continually reflected on why I hadn't developed the more assertive parts of my personality. I remembered my spiritual companion's words that I was extremely capable and I was not working at my full potential. I began to believe that God was confirming my life, that my life rejoiced the life of God and my suffering moved God to compassion.

Because I had no one to rely on or to make decisions for me, I was forced to face the specific realities of my life and grow up. The retreat was particularly helpful in this regard as it confirmed that I was gradually rebuilding my life story in a positive way. I listened very carefully to the words of advice my director had given me.

The director's responses helped me in the creation of my new story and opened me to the direction of God in my life. The most crucial response he made was in his attentive listening and deep care and concern for my well-being. He created an atmosphere of acceptance, trust and support yet encouraged independence. As I shared my story with him I came to realize the sacredness and uniqueness of these events. I came to know that God was co-creator in the events that unfolded. He was aware of my tone of voice, my body language and the messages not articulated. His responses helped me see patterns, emotions and conflicts and he pointed out in a supportive way parts of my personality that needed to be developed. He highlighted and brought forward different facets of the narrative and explored them with me, helping me

make connections that enabled me to begin to resolve difficulties. His comments and reassurance helped me discern that
God was working in my life and gave me guidance on how to
be in touch with his presence. He enabled me to grow in
self-knowledge by revealing patterns of behavior that were not
immediately obvious. When I found it difficult to talk, he
listened in such a way that welcomed my efforts. He helped
me see God's presence in the ordinary events of my life and to
become aware of how I was responding.

3

Understanding
and Spiritual Direction

In addition to being a narrative activity, spiritual direction is a hermeneutical process. The directee is engaged in a process of self-understanding in the light of his or her experience of God. The director is also involved in a hermeneutical process, namely, understanding the directee's account of his or her life story and experience of God. A narrative approach to spiritual direction can fruitfully be understood within the larger framework of hermeneutical theory proposed by Hans-Georg Gadamer.

As is evident from the preceding case studies, spiritual direction narratives are produced in a conversation with all of the to and fro of interchange that takes place in a conversation. Gadamer adopts the model of a conversation as a paradigm for describing what happens in the process of understanding. His analysis of the conditions of a genuine conversation is thus relevant to this discussion because the same conditions obtain in the spiritual direction conversation. It is both a genuine conversation and a process of understanding.

Two other elements in Gadamer's hermeneutical theory have particular relevance to this discussion of spiritual direction: his description of the role of tradition in understanding and his discussion of *phronesis* in Aristotle.

Conditions of a Conversation

The process of spiritual direction ordinarily takes place in a one-to-one relationship in which two people come together at mutually agreed upon intervals to focus on the spiritual life of the person seeking direction and to support that person's growth in the Christian life.[1] This encounter unfolds with the ordinary dynamics of a conversation. In his important work on hermeneutics, *Truth and Method,* Hans-Georg Gadamer argues that understanding involves a reciprocal relationship between the one trying to understand and the "text" to be understood which is analogous to the relationship between conversants in a conversation.[2] Thus, he uses the model of a genuine conversation as his preferred model for analyzing the process of understanding itself. Since the narrative moments in the spiritual direction process, which is the focus of this analysis, take place within the larger frame of an actual conversation, the characteristics of a real conversation also apply to spiritual direction.

Among the characteristics Gadamer elaborates are (a) the mutuality of the enterprise, (b) a question/answer structure, (c) a shared condition of "unknowing," (d) a non-adversarial climate, and (e) a specific subject matter of understanding.

From the outset, Gadamer emphasizes mutuality. Partners in a conversation do not talk at cross-purposes, but are engaged in a common project and so take care to ensure that the other person is following what is being said. If a person wants what is said to be understood by the other, the speaker tries to provide the necessary detail and connections from one point to another so the partner can "follow" the relationship of one idea to another or similarly follow the plot of a narrative. The one following is trying to receive the meaning the speaker communicates. Initially, questions serve the purpose of clarification and verification that the one following is understanding what the speaker means. What directs the course of the conversation is not one or other of the participants, but the subject matter of understanding to which the partners are directed in the conversation. Both partners are led by the subject they are pursuing together.

Not only is a conversation a mutual enterprise in the way it is conducted through the engagement with a common subject matter, but it is also mutual in a shared condition of "unknowing." Even the person supposedly leading the conversation is always ignorant to some degree because the outcome lies in what emerges from both participants. Both conversants are contributing to the process. Neither knows what will "come out" by the end. This indeterminacy is the shared condition of "unknowing" with which both participants enter the conversation.

This mutual openness to what emerges within the conversation is not necessarily a total indeterminacy. When one of the conversants in a dialogue has greater knowledge of a particular subject than the other, the less knowledgeable person can accede to the other. The directee may well recognize that the director is "superior . . . in judgment and insight and that for this reason his (her) judgment takes precedence."[3] This ascription of authority to the other is not based on the role the director plays but on actual knowledge which the directee recognizes that the other possesses. In Sam's case study, he alludes to this kind of deference to knowledge based on experience when he mentioned how his director's experience of community decision-making in her religious order was helpful to him. He described her as "having had her own battles." Specifically, she was able to help him understand something new about the decision-making process in regard to community housing that was frustrating to Sam from his perspective.

Progression in the conversation takes place in a non-adversarial climate. The mutuality of the enterprise requires a collaborative climate. What the partners seek to do is not to out-argue each other but to weigh one another's opinion—to test it out. This act of testing is the art of questioning. It seeks not to discover the weakness in the other's contribution but through the art of thinking to discover and welcome the real strength the other offers. Questioning at this stage seeks to find the common ground of truthful agreement which forms the basis of an emerging common meaning.

This search for the positive contribution of each partner is the question and answer dialectic Gadamer describes as an essential part of the structure of a genuine conversation. This process is a form of questioning that asks "Could this be the case? If so, how?" etc. What emerges from this kind of dialogue is a new "logos" which belongs to neither of the conversants individually but which transcends the subjective opinions of both partners. Working out such common meaning requires that they come under the influence of the truth of the subject they are pursuing together. This cannot be achieved if the participants are merely involved in self-expression and the successful assertion of their own viewpoints.[4]

Spiritual direction takes place under the same general conditions for conducting a "real" conversation. However, because the specific subject of understanding is the actual religious experience of the person seeking direction and the implications of this experience for the life of this person, the focus of the conversation, the shared subject of understanding, is what the person seeking direction presents from his or her experience. This conversation is mutual in the sense that both people are trying to understand what the directee is describing or explaining and that the conversants continue to seek to understand what the other is saying about this common subject matter. However, it is not a conversation that is necessarily mutual in the degree or kind of self-disclosure because the director usually does not offer personal experiences for mutual understanding in this conversation.

Likewise, the nature of religious experience itself places both the director and the directee in a condition of indeterminacy. The director cannot know better than the directee what is happening to the person. The director can invite the directee to understand and so more accurately interpret these kinds of experiences by exploring more fully some events more than others. But it seems characteristic of good spiritual direction sessions that both the director and the directee are surprised by the outcome of the conversation. Both the person seeking direction and the director are learners in this process.

In order for this kind of collaborative exploration to take place, a non-adversarial climate is also a feature of this conversation. Any significant form of self-disclosure about experiences or ideas which a person values deeply requires this receptive climate. In spiritual direction, this quality is particularly necessary so that the common subject matter of understanding can enter the conversation.

A question/answer structure of dialogue is another feature which is clearly operative in the spiritual direction conversation. Generally, the person seeking direction will establish the starting point or the initial subject matter for a particular session. Frequently, the subject matter of mutual understanding will take the form of the narration of one or several experiences that have occurred since the last conversation. Questions put to the person seeking direction may elicit either greater narrative detail such as an expansion of what happened, another narrative describing something from the person's history that would illuminate this incident, or some other linguistic form of explanation. These questions will be of both types referred to above: questions which serve to clarify and questions which search for truthful agreement. Thus, the narrative activity characteristic of spiritual direction occurs within the conversational mode and often emerges as the answer to questions arising within the conversation.

Role of Tradition

Gadamer claims that tradition is an element of freedom and of history. Tradition is part of human experience, affecting attitudes and behavior, not something outside.[5] The traditions which particularly inform the spiritual direction conversation are the Christian religious tradition and the western literary tradition. The relationship of spiritual direction to these traditions is complex and multifaceted. As is evident from Chapter One, the fact that men and women currently engage in the process of spiritual direction is in direct continuity with a specific Christian tradition that honors spiritual direction as an important means for encouraging spiritual growth.

The influence of this tradition is even more profound than simply a continuity of pastoral praxis. The Christian tradition itself is characteristically narrative in its scriptures, worship, and catechesis.[6]

The story-telling that takes place within the spiritual direction conversation is already contextualized within a "storied" tradition which forms the consciousness of the contemporary storyteller through the shared story of Jesus and salvation history which reaches back into the narratives of the Hebrew scriptures and strains forward through the age of the church to the end times themselves.

This particular religious tradition, which continues to express its shared faith through story and ritual, ascribes religious significance to the personal history of the individual as well as to the community because of the consistent conviction that the God-human encounter takes place in and through human history. The entire biblical tradition expresses both a shared experience and vision of the God-human relationship, namely, that God offers a relationship to God's self that is conducted over time and that respects human freedom and growth. Narrative is the linguistic form which best communicates this kind of experience. It is no surprise that the biblical authors were among the first to develop the skills of prose fiction because their theological perspective required it.

Robert Alter in his sensitive treatment of the art of narrative in the Hebrew scriptures makes the same point that the very nature of the God-human relationship could only be most effectively rendered through what he calls a "fictionalized" history. Only through developing the resources of prose fiction could the sacred writers depict their religious vision with both the precision and subtlety demanded by their subject.

He describes a tendency to "fictionalize" history in biblical narratives in order to represent the reality of the God-human relationship most effectively.

> The implicit theology of the Hebrew Bible dictates a complex moral and psychological realism in biblical narrative because God's purposes are always entrammeled in history, dependent on the acts of individual men and women for their continuing realization. To scrutinize biblical personages as fictional characters is to see them more sharply in the multifaceted, contradictory aspects of their human individuality, which is the biblical God's chosen medium for his experiment with Israel and history.[7]

Although not every narrative technique used by Semitic authors found its way into the western literary tradition, it has long been accepted that the literary form of prose fiction established by biblical authors exerted a profound influence on the subsequent development of fiction in the west.[8] As a consequence, both a narrative religious tradition and a secular literary tradition combine to provide the religious and cultural context for producing a certain form of personal narrative in spiritual direction.

The narrative form, originating in Christian experience, which most directly influences the spiritual direction narrative is the invention of spiritual autobiography in the *Confessions of St. Augustine*. Augustine adopts the literary form of the journey from Roman prose, a narrative of dramatic outer events, and uses it to describe the drama and intensity of the growth and development of his inner life.[9] Augustine manages to shift the drama of salvation history to its microcosmic form as it is played out in an individual human person. This shift to the individual's narrative expresses the Christian conviction of the unique worth and value of every human person because God chooses to be concerned with each of us. Spiritual direction encourages an oral narration of such personal accounts of salvation history.

The role tradition plays in spiritual direction is rather complex. In the process of understanding and interpreting experience, the "traditions" in which the director and the person seeking direction stand are constantly operative. Gadamer helps to illumine the greater complexity of the relationship to tradition in his analysis of the role of "prejudice," "horizon of meanings," and tradition in the process of understanding.

Gadamer asserts that when a person is engaged in understanding something, there is, of necessity, a process of bringing one's pre-understandings to bear on the current experience. A person projects some meaning for the whole as soon as some initial meaning begins to emerge. That initial meaning emerges only because one has some kind of expectation. However, one is always constantly revising these pre-conceptions or expectations on the basis of what is actually emerging.

For Gadamer, then, "prejudices," or pre-understandings, are not essentially negative, but are a necessary condition for understanding to occur at all. However, these "prejudices" or fore-conceptions must be replaced by more suitable ones in the process of remaining open to the meaning of the other person or the text. They exist then as anticipatory ideas and need to be made conscious when the newness of what a person is trying to understand challenges the interpreter in some way. The subject matter of understanding must be able to assert its truth against these pre-understandings.[10] As a director listens to the story being told, he or she must continually revise these anticipated meanings in the light of the directee's actual unfolding story.

In the spiritual direction conversation, the director and the person seeking direction usually share a complex set of "prejudices" or pre-understandings which are derived not only from a common cultural heritage and a shared contemporary context, but also from the larger Christian tradition. Both people will have been shaped by this tradition in their spiritual life, practices, and theology. Because many of these "prejudices" are rooted in a common source and are shared by both people, it is possible to assert that the tradition itself provides a context of shared "prejudices." And insofar as both people are in tacit agreement about these shared "prejudices," they may never come explicitly to awareness in the conversation itself. These shared prejudices are only likely to become explicit if they prove inadequate in interpreting new experiences.

The fact that individuals share "prejudices" which derive from the tradition in which they stand simply indicates the historicality of human consciousness. These shared "prejudices" can actually form a horizon of common meaning. Gadamer discusses the concept of "horizon" of meaning in the context of historical consciousness and the limiting factor that the period of time in which one lives exerts on a person. A horizon is "the range of vision that includes all that can be seen from a particular vantage point."[11] Consequently, a text from an earlier period of history is limited in its horizon to its own period of history. The interpreter will need to distinguish his or her own horizon from that of the text and yet let these horizons fuse again to release present meaning. In attempting to understand something produced in another temporal horizon, one is constantly confronted with a to and fro movement. The interpreter attempts to appreciate the earlier horizon and yet also experiences a fusion of an earlier horizon with one's own so that a meaning for the present can emerge. In this fusion of horizons, the interpreter can never exit from one's own horizon. Rather, one's own horizon expands to include the horizon of the other.

Barrett J. Mandel offers an example of this kind of fusion of horizons in which meaning in the present emerges for the interpreter when he or she encounters a horizon different from one's own in reading autobiography.

> Often the reader simply cannot know whether what he is reacting to is actually implied by the text or whether the text has triggered associations in the reader's own horizon. But it is this very overlapping of the autobiographer's and the reader's horizons that adds to the undeniable aura of truthfulness surrounding the text. In fact, it may be said that the reader projects truthfulness from his or her own body of assumptions or that he or she allows the text to manifest itself at the level of the truth.
>
> . . . For me these profound moments body forth a sense of my sharing life—being—with the author, no matter how remote he or she may be from me in some ways. The autobiographer springs open a door and gives me a glance into his or her deepest reality, at the same time casting my mind into a state of reverie or specula-

tion. . . . It is the moment Teresa of Avila experiences when she reads the garden scene in St. Augustine's *Confessions:* "When I began to read the *Confessions,* I thought I saw myself there described, and began to recommend myself greatly to this glorious Saint. When I came to his conversion, and read how he heard that voice in the garden, it seemed to me nothing less than that our Lord had uttered it for me: I felt so in my heart, I remained for some time lost in tears, in great inward affliction and distress." At such a moment, St. Teresa's language merges with that of St. Augustine who seems to be speaking not only *to* her but *in* her, merging the particulars of his past with the particulars of hers and creating a moment of transcendence.[12]

In the spiritual direction conversation, both participants are likely to share a common temporal horizon. However, both people may encompass a more or less narrow or broad horizon even in the present, and, consequently, need to distinguish these from one another in order to maximize their mutual understanding. However, one not only distinguishes these personal horizons, but they may also fuse just as Teresa's did with Augustine's in a moment of insight.

In addition, since all human life lives out of the horizon of the past which exists in the form of tradition, there is an historical dimension within every contemporary horizon of meaning. To become conscious of this reality in one's own consciousness is to acquire an historical horizon, the ability to situate one's present in relationship to the tradition or the history out of which one's own present emerges.[13]

In the spiritual direction conversation, either partner in the dialogue may have a greater or lesser facility for situating a given issue in spiritual direction within an appropriate historical context of the spiritual tradition(s). One would hope that a spiritual director would have sufficient knowledge of the history of spirituality and the variety of experiences and recorded wisdom within this tradition to be of help to the person seeking direction in achieving an appropriate horizon in which to explore a concrete situation in the directee's life.

The tradition not only ascribes religious significance to the personal history of an individual and provides a shared horizon of understanding for both the director and the person seeking direction, but it also exists in a reciprocal relationship with the individuals who stand within it. Individuals not only stand within a tradition and are shaped by it in their attitudes and their behaviors, but individuals also address questions to the tradition. "Tradition is not simply a precondition into which we come, we produce it ourselves, inasmuch as we understand, participate in the evolution of tradition and hence further determine it ourselves."[14] Thus people, reflecting on their experiences in the present context of spiritual direction, are capable of asking questions of the tradition and are not simply determined by the claims of the existing tradition. This aspect of the reciprocal relationship of people to the tradition in which they stand is especially important in an historical period like our own in which reflection on certain forms of contemporary experience seeks to either renew or reform a tradition. For example, that which has been handed on to us in the Christian tradition has not adequately assimilated or preserved the contribution of women to the ongoing formation of the tradition because of what feminist analysis names the patriarchal and androcentric bias which governed the traditioning process itself.[15] Although women's experience is better represented in the mystical tradition than in other traditions within Christianity, their contributions usually entered the tradition only through male sponsorship and/or censorship and consequently may not encompass the full range of experience of even these remarkable women. The contemporary experience of spiritual direction may eventually be a means of contributing to the overall tradition as it incorporates the actual religious experience of both women and men, lay, religious, and clerical, married and single. If, as Gadamer claims, one's relationship with the tradition is truly reciprocal, that is, one is not only addressed by the tradition but also shapes it, then new strands of the spiritual tradition may well emerge out of the contemporary situation.

Practical Knowledge

Finally, Gadamer emphasizes that understanding the tradition in which one stands requires that one must understand it in different ways. "Understanding is, then, a particular case of the application of something universal to a particular situation."[16] Treating the question of how this process functions, Gadamer draws on Aristotle's analysis of *phronesis,* practical knowledge, to show how one operates in a practical, moral way.[17] The practice of spiritual direction requires a similar kind of ability to recognize what is required in a particular situation.

Aristotle distinguishes between theoretical knowledge and practical knowledge. Practical knowledge is the kind of knowledge that one acquires in and through action, through participation and engagement. It is acquired in the process of character development. It is also more than *techne* or a skill. A skill can be acquired and forgotten. *Phronesis* is not something which can be forgotten because it is part of one's development.

The person is always in a situation of having to act and so must possess and be able to apply a practical knowledge to the situation. But *phronesis* is not something one has. What is right or appropriate can only be fully determined within the situation which requires action. One learns to see in a situation a need for action, action to be performed in the light of what is right. This kind of "seeing" is a knowing which embraces both the means and the end. Its opposite is blindness, an inability to recognize that a situation calls for action of a moral nature. This kind of knowledge exemplifies for Gadamer the way in which application is integral to understanding itself. If one cannot make an appropriate application, one really does not understand. In the case of practical knowledge, one doesn't first master principles and then apply them. Rather application co-determines understanding as a whole from the beginning.

The understanding (both that of the director and that of the directee) in the spiritual direction conversation is one that is eminently practical. Among other things, directees want to understand what is required of them in the concrete situation of their unique circumstances. In this case what is required is not restricted simply to the morally good thing to do as in Aristotle's discussion of ethics as related to *phronesis*. In spiritual direction directees are not only confronted with choices about the morally good, but also with choices among morally good things to do or ways of responding in particular situations. What directees are seeking to do is to understand and respond to that to which they experience God calling/inviting them through the whole of their graced religious histories and life circumstances.

In Sam's case, one instance of the exercise of this kind of practical knowledge was whether or not he wanted to apply for presbyteral ordination in the context of Jesuit life.[18] In order to arrive at his decision, he had to reflect on his history in the Society of Jesus, the consistent experience of relatedness to God through the whole of his time in the Society, and his desire to respond to this concretely experienced invitation. His experience at the diaconal ordination ceremony which he relates in the case study was one typical example of the pattern of call and response as he experienced it. Secondly, he had to rule out reasons for making this decision that might have been motivated by fear or some other lack of freedom. This he did by placing his choice for ordination in contrast with a choice to live as a married man in a happy family. In this way, he could discover that his choice for celibate ordination in community was not motivated primarily by fear of a life option that was repugnant to him.

He also needed to rule out any hesitation in proceeding to ordination based on psychological constraints. His strong desire/need to "be ready" was a need to be in control of his life beyond what was necessary at this time. This dynamic he confronted by exploring some of the contributing causes to this feeling and realizing that they were not persuasive. Finally, he needed to reflect on what was happening in psychoanalysis and judge whether or not any of the issues he was confronting there would have suggested either delaying the decision or questioning his deeper vocational motivation.

It was precisely the narrative detail Sam presented about his experience that made it possible for the director to grasp the particular circumstances of his situation and the choices facing him. Once she could understand this, she could facilitate Sam's development of his own *phronesis* in the context of his experience.

In Mary's case, she wonders if she should become a religious when her marriage failed. Her director, from his practical knowledge of her and others, laughed because this possibility was clearly incongruous for Mary and probably a fantasy of escape from her situation. Mary learned something about the principle of Ignatian discernment which cautions against making decisions in a condition of desolation from this episode.

That kind of participation in another's life originates from the bond established between the director and the directee which assumes that the director is "friendly" to the directee. Being "friendly" means that the director is seeking what the directee wants most deeply, to do what he or she believes God wants. The director thus "thinks with the other and undergoes the situation with him or her."[19] This capacity to undergo a situation with another is frequently achieved through imaginative participation in the other's narrative.[20]

One of the goals of spiritual direction is to support the directee's growth in the spiritual life, helping him or her to become the person he or she desires to be. This can only be accomplished within the concrete particulars of each person's life. As the director works with different people, he or she gradually develops *phronesis,* knowledge acquired for oneself, as he or she responds to the concrete situation presented by each directee. The director thus develops a form of practical knowledge in the way he or she functions as a director.

Gadamer makes another point in relationship to *phronesis* which is relevant to the situation of spiritual direction. *Phronesis* is characterized not only by the interplay between principles and their application but also by the interplay between the goal of becoming a good person and embodying that in one's life. This dialectical interplay is an ongoing, self-revising process. One's ability to imagine what the good person would do is based both on one's experience of other people as well as on one's ideal of the virtuous person. Only by succeeding in behaving virtuously can one truly understand why that way of acting is virtuous and what its effects are on the moral agent.

In spiritual direction, the director is engaged both in the process of becoming a good person as well as encouraging similar development in directees. The director will somehow embody virtuous qualities, such as reverence, patience, or fairness, within the spiritual direction relationship. Only by being patient, for instance, in this situation as well as in others will the director be able to understand and evaluate the progress of character development in directees.

Through the course of this chapter, the relevance of Gadamer's hermeneutical theory for spiritual direction has been elaborated. Spiritual direction is clearly a hermeneutical situation, a situation in which a process of understanding is constantly transpiring. The directee is seeking to understand and interpret religiously significant experiences in relationship to his or her life story and the tradition which informs this understanding. The director is facilitating the directee's self-understanding through the ability to understand the directee's story. The conditions of conducting a genuine conversation are applicable to the actual conversation conducted in spiritual direction as well as serving as a model for how one understands. Finally, understanding in spiritual direction always has a practical goal and is a form of practical knowledge.

It now remains to be seen in the following chapter why the narrative moments in the spiritual direction conversation are of such major importance.

4

Narrative and Human Experience

Chapter Three situated the interpretive activity occurring in spiritual direction in an hermeneutical framework. Because directees do tell their stories in spiritual direction, this chapter describes the characteristics of narrative and its relationship to human experience. Narrative is the linguistic form most related to the way people maintain a sense of continuity through time and a primary form in which they share experience. Understanding the nature of narrative and its importance is the first step for appreciating why a narrative approach to spiritual direction is logical, desirable and beneficial.

Without evaluating the range of narrative theologians and other thinkers interested in the role and nature of narrative, I have chosen a few themes which contribute to an understanding of narrative in the spiritual direction conversation. The theorists whose contributions are most important for this discussion are Stephen Crites, John Shea, George Stroup, Robert Alter, Eric Auerbach, Michael Novak, Robert Scholes, Robert Kellogg, Paul Ricoeur, Northrup Frye, James Hillman, Philip Wheelwright, and Michael Polanyi.[1]

Defining Narrative

I am using the conceptual category of "narrative" as a heuristic tool for identifying the narrative aspects in the process of spiritual direction. In this sense, one can analyze some of the characteristic interactions between the director and the person seeking direction as a narrative situation within a conversational mode in which the directee narrates his or her life experiences in the context of faith. The director is both audience and interlocutor. As an interlocutor, the director influences the narration of the other's experience both by how she or he enters into the conversation and by non-verbal responses.[2]

The person seeking direction usually produces a life story narrative governed by the purpose of spiritual direction, the seriality of these conversations, and an oral form of narration. These factors give the narrative distinctive features which will be described further in Chapter Six.

The narration of experience does not exclude all other forms of discourse in spiritual direction. Rather, the life story provides a major context for interpreting the non-narrative forms of discourse which may occur in spiritual direction, such as meditation, doxology, theological discussion or the presentation of insight that arises from intuitive, contemplative perceptions. Conceptualizing spiritual direction as a narrative process allows one to identify the role of narrative in this interaction, examine some of its effects on both the narrator and the director, and reflect on the implications of this narrative process for the practice of spiritual direction.

Minimally, a narrative is a symbolic presentation of events, connected by subject matter in the judgment of the speaker, related by time, and offered by the narrator to either an actual or an implied audience.[3] Most people, however, have more complex expectations of narrative. They expect (1) some form of temporal sequencing, which connects events causally as well as chronologically or in some other recognizable pattern, (2) some reference to character and the world of human values, and (3) meaning or significance. Traditional literary criticism has developed the terminology of plot, character, theme, and narrative strategies such as point of view, tone, author's voice, irony, and imagery to account for and to describe these distinguishable elements of narrative.[4]

In addition to sequence and pattern in narrative forms, narratives also incorporate into their structure elements of explanation and description. Although these elements are non-narrative in form, both description and explanation are frequently incorporated into narratives. Their presence in a narrative is assimilated into the narrative experience as a whole. Descriptive sections invite the reader/listener to co-create the setting or character by imagining what is being described following the clues of the narrator. For example, one imagines what a character looks like or what a given setting is like. As such, description draws the reader/listener cooperatively into the tale.

When a person describes an experience, descriptive detail often reveals attitudes, feelings, and habits of responding to life experiences. Thus, the descriptive model discloses the narrator's "point of view."[5] Narrative description allows another to share the unique way he or she experiences life. Spiritual direction is largely concerned with the response of the person seeking direction to religious experience and how that experience affects the person's perceptions and responses to life. The directee's style and content of description and explanation allow the director to observe such changes in the directee's perceptions.

Likewise, narrative assimilates explanation into the experience. Two different forms of explanation, emplotment and formal argument, occur in narrative. Plot is its own form of explanation. The shape of a plot in both its sequence and pattern offers an explanation of why things turn out as they do.[6] To this "explanation by emplotment," normal explanation is often added.[7]

Spiritual direction conversations frequently contain both

types of explanation. Directees embody their explanatory theories in the plots of their narratives as well as offering direct explanation. James Hillman asserts that in psychoanalytic case histories, which he describes as fictions, "plots are our theories. They are the ways in which we put the intentions of human nature together so that we can understand the *why* between the sequence of events in story."[8]

This correlation between theory and emplotment suggests that any theory, not just a psychoanalytic one, can be woven into the spiritual direction narrative through the combination of plot and narrator-offered explanation. For instance, theological theories such as the person's view of divine providence will be incorporated into the narrative detail of the plot itself. How God's activity is influencing the events and relationships of a person's life will be narrated as an element of the plot.

Conversely, the interpretive theories of the director will affect his or her response to the directee's stories. If the director's guiding theory is theological, she or he is likely to identify for the directee the theological dimension related to the story just heard. The director might make a comment such as, "Your story seems to be about experiences of God's providential care surrounding your life." If the listener to such a story is influenced by a Jungian psychological theory, the same tale might be identified as an experience of "synchronicity." Either interpretive response will then affect how future stories are narrated and explained in the conversation.

In summary, narrative or story as used in this study is discourse characterized by a temporal sequence of events or actions, organized in a pattern, disclosing a point of view, and connected by subject matter. Explanation and description belong to narrative when they are placed within the narrative context.

Regardless of the way different theorists describe the relationship between narrative activity and life experience, there is a relationship between fictional worlds and the world of human experience. Narrational patterns both mirror life patterns and inform those less easily perceived patterns of life with greater coherency of form. When human lives are compared to a story, the assertion is often made that people are stories. Their beginning is marked by birth and their end by death. And the events of a person's life are connected by both temporal sequencing and cause-effect relationships. People find themselves

> . . . in situations that they change or to whose changes they react. These changes in turn reveal hidden aspects of the situation and the characters of the people and give rise to a new predicament calling for thought or action or both. The response to this predicament brings the story to its conclusion.[9]

The sense that a human life is itself a story assumes that life has or can be made to have a sense of continuity over a lifetime. Michael Novak suggests that "story" is a means of achieving continuity: "A story is a structure for time. A story links actions over time. The more integrated a life, the more all things in it work toward a single (perhaps comprehensive) direction. The richer the life, the more subplots the story encompasses."[10]

People, then, enact a story by their actions which, when linked together in an internal narrative, create the continuity of personal identity. This sense of personal identity is itself a narrative construction, and its relevance to spiritual direction will be taken up in Chapter Five.

Now that a working definition for narrative has been established, it is necessary to examine the relationship between narrative form and human experience. Why do persons in spiritual direction initially attempt to communicate their life experiences in narrative form? Narrative form is related to the human experience of oneself in time. Past, present, and future all co-inhere.

Stephen Crites' analysis of the narrative quality of experience shows just how fundamental narrative is. He argues that consciousness itself must have a narrative form corresponding to narrative forms of discourse common to all cultures.[11] Narrative activity is not optional for human subjects. Consciousness is narrative. People learn to articulate their own narratives because they live within a culture which provides them with particular narrative models. Even personal and cultural identities are narrative constructions. Experiences that are transformative, that alter one's vision of reality, require the creation of an identity narrative which can integrate past and future with these experiences. Spiritual direction is one situation which encourages individuals to grasp the coherence and significance of their religious experience and its impact on the whole of their personal histories partially through narrating it.

The Narrative Quality of Experience

In his important essay, "The Narrative Quality of Experience," Stephen Crites argues that "the formal quality of experience through time is inherently narrative."[12] This narrative quality of experience is rooted in the essential historicality of the experiencing subject.

The fact that we organize our lives through stories is not unlike the experience of music. Each event, each note occurs in temporal succession and is experienced as a unity only through time. The resulting form is "revealed only in the action as a whole."[13] In verbal structures, narrative is the form "capable of expressing coherence through time."[14]

Further, Crites argues that we engage in this narrative organization of experience not only because temporal consciousness requires it, but also because this consciousness is continually shaped by a storied sense of reality. Somehow we live in stories too deep to tell before we bring our own or our culture's to explicit articulation.[15] For consciousness to mediate between a narrative shaping of consciousness and our individual and collective elaboration of narratives, consciousness, too, must be narrative in form,[16] a result of our experience of ourselves in time.

This temporality is experienced through the always interrelated model of time past, present, and future. Only the present actually exists, but it exists only in a correlative relationship to its past and future.[17] Before one can understand the complex relationship of these tensed modalities of past, present, and future, it is necessary to look at both the simple and the complex functions of memory which partially account for a narrative form of consciousness.

Memory in its simplest form gives coherence to the momentary precepts, feelings, and thoughts that constitute experience by preserving temporal succession. Without this temporal connection, all experience would be locked into a fragmentary present unconnectable to past or future. At first there is a simple preservation of an image stream which is ordered only by temporal succession.[18] No other operation than simply recalling something from it is often performed. In a sense there is something "there" to be consulted when someone needs to place an event in its sequence, much the way one retraces a sequence of activities in looking for a lost article.

However, memory is more complex than simple recall. Memory is also able to recollect the images lodged in memory into constantly new patterns and reorderings of past experiences. To tell a story drawing from one's image-stream requires more than a recital of the chronicle of memory. Narrating a story, selecting a key episode from memory, is one of the most common ways of recollecting an experience from memory. In order to clarify this distinction between consulting the temporally sequenced image-stream and the more complex operations of "recollection" which offer constantly new interpretations in the retelling of an experience, Crites offers this example:

> I recall, for example, a sequence from my own memory. In telling its course, recollection already intervenes, but I recollect in a way as faithful as possible to memory itself. I measure out "a long time" and recall an episode from my childhood. I have not thought about it for many years, and yet I find its chronicle in good condition, extremely detailed and in clear sequence. In an impetuous fit of bravado I threw a rock through a garage window. I recall the exact spot on the ground from which I picked up the rock. I recall the wind-up, the pitch, the rock in midair, the explosive sound of the impact, the shining spray of glass, the tinkling hail of shards falling on the cement below, the rough, stony texture of the cement. I recall also my inner glee at that moment, and my triumph when a playmate, uncertain at first how to react, looked to me for his cue and then broke into a grin. Now I could cut and splice a bit, passing over hours not so clearly recalled anyway, except that my mood underwent drastic change. Then I recall that moment in the evening when I heard my father's returning footsteps on the porch and my guilty terror reached a visceral maximum the very memory of which wrenches a fat adult belly—for remembering is not simply a process in the head. The details of the scene that ensued are likewise very vivid in my memory.
> Now it would be quite possible for me to tell this story very differently. My perspective on it has been changed, partly by the death of my father and the fact that I am now myself the father of children, partly, too, by my

reading in the *Confessions* a story about a wanton theft of pears and by some reading in Freud on the rivalry of fathers and sons, and so forth. So I have many insights into this chronicle that I could not have had at the time its events occurred. Yet the sophisticated new story I might tell about it would be superimposed on the image-stream of the original chronicle. It could not replace the original without obliterating the very materials to be recollected in the new story. Embedded in every sophisticated retelling of such a story is this primitive chronicle preserved in memory. Even conscious fictions presuppose its successive form, even when they artfully reorder it.[19]

A second aspect of the narrative form of consciousness is the constantly experienced relationship between past, present, and future. These three modalities of time are present and related to one another in every moment of experience. The present exists only in relationship to the past out of which the present emerges and also exists in relationship to the future which the present can anticipate.

The elemental narrative form for the future corresponding to the narrative form of memory for the past can be called the "scenario of anticipation." By projecting courses of action, one imagines a variety of possible stories about the future. These future scenarios lack the density of detail in stories of the past, and often the future turns out differently from the projected stories. However, the anticipated scenario is related to the remembered past, especially through the sense of the self projected into the future. This sense of self which has continuity with the self in the past and present is a person's narratively constructed identity.

Although there is continuity between the past and the future, these temporal modes of experience are also clearly distinct from one another. The past has a determinacy about it. It is completed; its events and actions cannot be undone on the level of factual deed. The past can only be changed in the present through a reinterpretation or retelling based on new experience in the present.[20] Conversion stories are classical examples of retelling and reinterpreting the past based on an experience or understanding that was not available to the person during the actual events of the past. Augustine in the *Confessions* clearly retells the whole of his life from his newly assimilated perspective of Christian faith. The significance of past events may change but not the events. Just as the past is determinate, the future anticipated is as yet indeterminate.

Even though the past continues to determine experience in the present without conscious reference to memory,[21] only the present of things present exists as the decisive moment in an unfolding story because the present constitutes the moment of action in relationship to past and future. The narrative quality of experience only takes place in the present moment. It is in and from the present that we remember the past, experience present reality, and anticipate the future. However, the present is also the temporal and physical location of embodied human experience which constitutes the nature and structure of our experience.[22]

Narratives can only be produced through bodily instrumentality. The communication which takes place between director and directee is always immediately embodied. The directee as narrator gives voice to his or her story and employs non-verbal body language as well as words to express experience. Facial expression, physical movement, voice, eye contact, physical sensations related to affect all contribute to the communication process.

For instance, the way in which directees enter the room and sit down expresses how they are indwelling their world this day and how safe or trusting they feel in the director's presence. One person I saw for direction took eight months to move from the far cushion on the couch to the seat directly

facing my chair. I took this gradual change in physical posi-
tioning to indicate increasing trust and comfortableness with
himself and me in the direction process.

Finally, as Crites demonstrated in his story of breaking a
garage window, feelings, in his case remembered ones, are
known and expressed in a physical way. In spiritual direction,
feelings become present in a fully embodied way as people tell
a story of past experience. The feelings in the present telling
are not necessarily identical with the remembered ones. The
directee experiences reactions to the narrated events which are
frequently first known and experienced physically before they
become verbalized.

This process of communication and interaction is fully
embodied for both persons. The director is also experiencing
the directee and responding in a physical way. The director
receives the directee's story through bodily perception. And
the director comes to rely on a felt bodily sense of the person's
narrative in and through an embodied form of knowing.

In summary, according to Crites, the experiencing consciousness itself has a narrative form rooted in the temporality
of human consciousness. This consciousness mediates between the stories which shape it and the stories produced by
this already narrative consciousness. To say that consciousness is narrative in form is not to say that consciousness is
exclusively narrative in form, but that the temporality of
human experiencing corresponds to the narrative forms that
cultures develop to express it.

Life imitates art and art imitates life. The narrative form
of consciousness is far more rudimentary in pattern and sequence than is any articulated narrative. The more tightly
organized plots and motifs of artful narratives help give
greater coherence to the more inchoate pattern and sequence
of a person's consciousness.[23] People do not acquire their
stories in an ahistorical, isolated manner but from the culture

in which they dwell. Michael Novak puts it this way. "How does one acquire a story? The culture in which one is born already has an image of time, of the self, of heroism of ambition, of fulfillment. It burns its heroes and archetypes deeply into one's psyche."[24]

It is now clear that narrative forms are never replaced by other linguistic forms because narrative is so intimately rooted in the historicality of our consciousness.

Narrative and Metaphorical Expression of Experience

Experience

Most people naturally adopt a narrative mode when they share an experience. Human experience is an interpretive encounter with someone or something and a reflective, conceptual awareness of this encounter. As Denis Edwards defines it:

> Experience is best seen as encounter with some thing or person which has become available to consciousness through reflective awareness. It refers to an encounter that is interpreted within human consciousness. This second element, interpretation, has always already occurred whenever we know we have experienced something.[25]

According to this definition, the interpretive element does not occur in a moment of subsequent reflection, but the "interpreting self precedes the encounter, enters into the encounter, and reflects upon the encounter."[26]

Experiences which affect us deeply require subsequent reflection and interpretation to assimilate their effects and to grasp their implications. This subsequent reflection is dependent upon the "richly nuanced totality in which experience, thought and interpretation run together in the same way as past, present and expectations of the future."[27] One is always capable of distinguishing between the original experience and the later reflection. There is frequently the sense that the original experience is too rich to be accounted for adequately in conceptual expression.

Phenomenologically, human experience is of such variety that there are sensory, conceptual, and skill factors involved. In any given experience one of these will tend to predominate although the other factors may also be present. The mode of experiencing reality most important to this discussion is the "tacit," pre-conceptual, or skill mode.[28]

Michael Polanyi develops the notion of "tacit" knowing or experiencing by reflecting on the forms of knowing entailed in performing a craft. Skills cannot be apprehended or conveyed in concepts alone. Much of what is genuinely known in the practical performance of a task cannot be told.[29]

Experiences of love, beauty, music, and God are examples of such experiences which occur in the skill mode. These cannot be reduced to concepts or words. To speak about such experiences one uses concepts, images, and words, but something in the experience remains beyond the ability to verbalize it. The experience of the beauty of a piece of music transcends the sounds themselves and the structure of the music which can be grasped conceptually. The apprehension of beauty in the music results from the individual aspects as well as from the experience of it as a whole. The whole is more than the sum of the parts. The apprehension of beauty is experienced in a pre-conceptual form—a form of awareness that is not conceptual. What is ordinarily called an experience of God is usually a pre-conceptual mode of knowing, an awareness of God that is limited neither to sensory nor to intellectual factors, but is nonetheless present in awareness.

In summary, experience is always interpreted, a complex interaction among sensory, conceptual, and pre-conceptual factors. Some of the elements of interpretation find their basis directly in the experience itself and other elements of interpretation are brought to us from elsewhere, at the very least from outside this experience.[30] Experience is an encounter with someone or something, a reality which may be external to the self, which can become available to consciousness. Experience of itself has a temporal quality to it; to become "experienced" is a process which takes place in a cumulative fashion through time.

Expressing Experience

How do people ordinarily go about sharing an experience? To the question "What happened or what was your experience?" the most frequent response is a story of the experience. The narrator tells what she or he experienced, usually including the thoughts about the event and the feelings evoked by it in some form of temporal sequence. Narrating an event is the usual way in which people witness to the reality of their experience. Through its narrative representation, the auditor is invited to participate imaginatively in the experience and judge its plausibility. Effective narration is one method a person uses to persuade an auditor of the truth of the narrator's assertion about the event in question.[31]

Some examples might make this clearer. Narrative is the usual form for communicating the "news." Even in our highly visual culture, all news coverage must contain what happened to someone at a specific time and place and offer some reason why the event occurred. Effort is made to reconstruct a plausible set of events in temporal sequence to explain, if not why something happened, at least how it happened. All reportage is narrative in this rudimentary way. Narrative form is, then, the ordinary way people share an experience or report its actuality. Narrative is the form that best accounts for the unfolding through time of an experience or series of events that are related to each other.

The spiritual direction dialogue tends to encourage the narrative rendering of the directee's experience. It is one situation within the community of faith that honors a person's unique and specific experiences of faith. When directees narrate the events of their lives in which they experience the way the mysteries of faith are operative for them, their experience of faith becomes increasingly specific, coherent, personal, and concrete.

Narrative, by its nature, invites the imaginative participation of its hearers in the events narrated. It can offer opportunities for new experiences to the auditors as well as concretize those experiences for the narrator. Narrative is a primary form of communicating a tradition even as narratives of original experiences of faith embody that tradition anew or challenge it to change.

In spiritual direction people articulate experiences which are often difficult to relate. The directee may discover the religious dimension of reality operative in any realm of ordinary experience. Frequently, the directee's consciousness of the way God is present is very subtle and elusive. At other times, the approach of God is dramatic and impossible to ignore. How might one best express these often diverse experiences?

The spiritual director can facilitate the articulation and appropriation of these experiences by selectively eliciting narratives which portray these interactions between God and the directee. The purpose of this narrative activity is first to help the directee notice what is transpiring in the God-human relationship.[32] Once the directee can articulate what is happening, the second step is to explore the implications of this now concrete interaction for the directee.

Narrative form encourages the directee to disclose the event in chronological order incorporating the person's thoughts, feelings, actions, and reactions. Incoherence or confusion in the narrative indicates what in the experience has not yet been appropriated or sufficiently understood to produce a clear and precise narrative. It is a series of clues within the verbal composition and its oral delivery, e.g. voice tone, pauses, groping for words, rushes of words, which guides the director in deciding what aspects require comment, analysis, or elicitation of more detail.

The oral and spontaneous nature of these narratives tends to give them a diffuse character. Although the directee does select and shape the stories, material that would most likely be omitted in a written or rehearsed oral composition stays in the narrative and remains available for development or explication.

Finally, a given segment of a spiritual direction narrative retains its dependence on the narrator. The current experience is interpreted narratively and analytically within the context of the directee's life story. Although this life story is only partially articulated in spiritual direction, it remains a primary interpretive framework for the directee.

Some people may argue that lyric poetic form is equally or more suited for the expression of experience, especially religious experience, than is narrative. In my experience of spiritual direction, I do not find this form to be the primary mode of expression although some directees do offer a poem, a graphic representation, or a musical composition related to a single significant experience. Lyric poetry is particularly well-suited to express an intense experience of brief duration.[33]

However, I find the selective nature of these artistic forms less helpful than narrative in the initial exploration of an experience in spiritual direction. The tightly unified expression of lyric form excludes all seemingly extraneous or unintegrated details of an experience which do not contribute to the dominant effect the poet emphasizes. As a result of this conscious selectivity, the director lacks access to aspects of the experience the directee was unable to assimilate or adequately interpret.

Limitations of poetic or other artistic forms in the context of spiritual direction do not mean they cannot play an important role for the directee. I find such non-narrative forms of expression most useful after an initial exploration of the experience. These forms of expression then become a way of crystallizing the most significant aspect of the experience which may be clarified after the attempt to narrate it. Lyric or graphic expression becomes a way of appropriating the experience more deeply in an imaginative and synthetic way. An example from an actual spiritual direction conversation may help to demonstrate my preference for narrative over a lyric form of expression in the exploration of an experience.

A sister in her early fifties was making a week-long directed retreat. The third or fourth day of the retreat, instead of relating her experience since the previous day, Linda began reflecting on the gift of friendship with a priest. As she talked, she appeared shy and slightly flushed. Initially, the director was puzzled. Why had this topic emerged at this point in the retreat? What had evoked the memory of this friendship and her subsequent emotional and reflective preoccupation with it?

The director first invited a general description of the friendship. Linda described a pleasant, emotionally supportive relationship which entailed going out to dinner a couple of times and exchanging letters three or four times in a year. She had not seen her friend recently, nor did she frequently fantasize about him. The emotional intensity of Linda's relationship did not seem to account for her thinking about it most of the day. Nor did the director experience Linda's sexuality as particularly repressed although the topic had not become explicit yet.

When the director then asked her to describe what happened before she began to think about her friend, she related that she had been sitting under a tree, quietly attentive to God. In the midst of her prayer, she began to experience feelings of love and mild sexual sensations. It seemed to be this upsurge of gentle erotic and romantic feelings of love that had initiated the reverie and subsequent reflection about her friend.

Because Linda had never experienced or associated these kinds of feelings with prayer, she attributed them to her friendship. When the director suggested the possibility that her sexual feelings might have been a response to the loving and intimate quality of God's presence to her in the retreat, she began to relax and felt that might be true. She appeared to be less perplexed about her experience and shifted her attention away from her friend and back toward the God with whom she was involved. In the remainder of the retreat she became increasingly comfortable with her response to God's love.

If Linda had written a poem, its subject would probably have been friendship. On the evidence available in the poem, it would have been difficult for the director to uncover with Linda that part of her experience which she had not been able to understand.

This example illustrates one instance in which elaborating a narrative was partially responsible for the directee's ability to connect her meditation on the gift of friendship to the concrete feelings and events which initiated that reflection. In reconstructing the events narratively, Linda discovered for herself that she had mistaken the cause of her feelings. The director helped her find a more appropriate horizon in which to situate her experience by connecting her story to the mystical tradition, especially the writings of Teresa of Avila and John of the Cross. When Linda understood what had actually happened, she could respond more appropriately in the prayer experience as well as incorporate both experiences of love into a new narrative which accounted for these experiences more accurately.

This example clarifies the narrative moment in the spiritual direction conversation. In Linda's case, about half of this session was spent in elaborating a narrative that could explain why she was suddenly meditating on a relationship with an absent friend. The second half of the conversation depended on the content of the resulting narrative. This latter part of the conversation could be described as commentary on and discussion of the narrative.

Frequently, in the spiritual direction conversation, the directee shares a human experience of God. Because the person is talking about something that is pre-conceptual, the only way the directee can be concrete is to use imagery, metaphor, and symbol. A spiritual reality will be described in terms of other concretely experienced realities. Less difficult to articulate are the sensory, affective, and cognitive changes the person experiences as a result of these religious experiences. Directees necessarily employ figurative language in their narratives to express themselves.

Imagery, Metaphor, and Symbol

Imagery, metaphor, and symbol are words which have a variety of meanings in different contexts. I use the word "image" in two distinctly different ways. First, "image" may refer psychologically to the internal representation of a person, object, or scene in one's imagination. Second, in a linguistic utterance, an "image" is a verbal evocation of an object known from experience and its intended and suggested meanings and overtone.

The role of imagery in the spiritual direction conversation is related to the kinds of religious experience a particular directee has. For instance, some people regularly pray by using the classic method of "Ignatian Contemplation." In this form of prayer, the person creatively reconstructs in imagination the particular details of a Gospel story or an event in Christ's life.[34] For this kind of person, the images which occur in the prayer are the medium of the person's religious experience. This type of experience is one example of my first use of the term image. One cannot separate the imaging from the experience. The sense of the presence of God to this person and the affective quality of response is mediated through the person's imagination. Mary's narrative in Chapter Two gives us a hint of this kind of prayer. On the second day of the retreat she described the intensity of the pain which she brought to this scene. She began her prayer with an image of the crucifixion rather than with a Gospel text which is often used as the starting point for this type of prayer.

> The one event in Christ's life that could bear the weight of how I felt was the crucifixion. Prayer that day began in tears, darkness, silence. Then the image of Christ crucified began to take on much the same expression and scars my shattered face had. I came to know that my pain was his pain and his pain was mine. Scars that were bleeding on his face were also bleeding on mine, yet his eyes revealed a great capacity for love and constant hope. In his torn, weeping and rejected state he embraced me. I became still and dwelt waiting, for I felt I had nothing else. I began to abandon my own being and really trust in God.[35]

Later in the same day she described repeating use of this image with which she was identifying and through which she was being touched by grace. Most importantly, she was no longer isolated in her hurt, but gaining strength to bear it through experiencing Jesus with her in her pain.

A narrative produced after the prayer experience in the direction context will recount what the person saw, felt, understood, and did in the prayer which took this form of imaging. Conversation may spontaneously emerge between the Christ figure and the pray-er, or images entirely novel to a scriptural text used as a starting point may develop. In subsequent prayer experiences, the person may return to the imaged scene as Mary did and continue to let it develop and unfold.[36] Thus an imaged scene becomes the arena of the directee's ongoing encounter with God.[37]

The only way one can describe a contemplative experience of God which typically occurs without words, concepts, or images is through recourse to images or metaphoric language.[38] Some frequently occurring metaphors are drawn from the experience of darkness and light, especially the kind of light that is experienced as blinding and thus producing darkness. Gregory of Nyssa, Pseudo-Dionysius, the author of *The Cloud of Unknowing* and John of the Cross all draw on this metaphor in their characteristically apophatic mysticism.[39] Another set of metaphors comes from the experience of waking and sleeping, forgetfulness and oblivion.[40] Yet another set of metaphors is drawn from a love relationship between two people for other aspects of the experience.[41]

A third and very frequent occurrence of imagery in the spiritual direction conversation arises from the directee's attempt to articulate an experience which has some vagueness to it. If the directee can find an apt image, the experience becomes vivid and focused for the directee. Pam's case illustrates the emergence of such an image in the process of the direction conversation. The following is part of a direction session.

("P" represents Pam and "D" represents the director.)

P: The Lord and I are together, but it is as if we are on hold. So much has been happening, as you know. So much growth and discovering new things about myself. There's been so much that I feel I need a break. So the Lord and I are just quietly together. I feel I should be doing more, but I also need a rest. (Pam elaborates about her perceived growth, her desire for more, yet her need to be still for a while.)

D: You seem to be torn, Pam, about whether you should be "working" some more with yourself or taking it easy for a while. Have you shared your uncertainty with God?

P: Yes, and he's very relaxed about the whole thing. (Pause) He seems to be looking at the "new me," and I'm still looking at bits and pieces of me and trying to work out mistakes I've made. I sense he wants me to be a whole person. (Pause) Right now he seems to be stepping back and looking at the whole of my life. And he is asking me to do the same—to see my life from his perspective. He sees the whole picture and wants me to, also.

D: He would like you to see yourself and your life from his point of view as a unified whole . . .

P: Yes, that's right. (Pauses and seems to be noticing something) An image is coming to mind of a home-made woven rug we used to have in our living room when I was growing up. (Talking very slowly with pauses) The top is very smooth and all the threads are interwoven beautifully. They all fit together to make a beautiful rug. If you look underneath there are a lot of mistakes, rough edges, unevenness, loose black threads. (Pause)

The Lord is looking at my life from the top view
and asking me to see the pattern of my life, not the
loose ends. He desires me to accept my mistakes as an
important part of the interweaving of who I am today.
He says these have helped to give me depth and to tie
parts of my life together, just as the loose black threads
keep the rug fitted together.

And I keep wanting to look at the underneath
part of the rug, to work on parts of my life that need to
be dealt with: the loose threads and jagged edges. God
wants me to see how all the different parts of my life
and myself have been woven together into who I am
today.[42]

In Pam's case the image of the woven rug allows her to
clarify and distinguish among vague and confusing feelings
about an attitude toward herself she could adopt. In spiritual
direction, directees employ such images to express subtle
experiences in prayer and complex affective reactions or
feelings.

This reliance on metaphorical expression in the description of experience is neither affectively neutral nor innocent
of implications for behavior. When metaphorical images
function as symbols,

. . . they speak to man existentially and find an echo in
the inarticulate depths of his psyche. Such images communicate through their evocative power. They convey a
latent meaning that is apprehended in a nonconceptual,
even a subliminal way. Symbols transform the horizons of
man's life, integrate his perceptions of reality, alter his
scale of values, reorient his loyalties, attachments, and
aspirations in a manner far exceeding the powers of abstract conceptual thought. . . . They suggest attitudes and
courses of action; they intensify confidence and devotion.[43]

Wheelwright characterizes symbols by their permanence and stability, their rootedness in the cosmos, and their multivalence of meaning.[44] In this sense, the crucifixion could become a symbol for Mary of the presence of Christ to her in her pain and an offer of love and hope in the midst of it. It also carries more universal meanings within the Christian tradition.

By making explicit the latent meanings and logical implications of the dominant images and symbols which emerge in the spiritual direction conversation, one can discover the possible development of plot and affective attitudes implicit in this language. People are often telling more than they are able to grasp fully. Explicating the dominant symbols and pattern of imagery with people in direction can give them access to what they already know about themselves at some level. In Mary's case, an aspect of imagery that was never made explicit for her in direction was the way the landscape mirrored the interior movement of the retreat. In narrative terms, the symbolic role of setting was implicitly affecting her the whole time. She began by hiding in the rocks, in a cave overhung with growth, and gradually emerged into a night garden of delight and to more expansive open spaces. Her choice of setting for prayer and exploration was dictated unconsciously or semi-consciously by her movement from isolation to embrace, from hurt to comfort, from fear to trust.

The director can reinforce these symbols and intensify their effects on the person, change them by suggesting alternative scenarios or attitudes that the person might want to entertain toward events, or ignore them.

For example, Pam's developed image of the two sides of the rug seems to suggest that she could choose to change her preference for looking at what is wrong (the loose ends) to looking at what is good (the pattern from the top-side). In Mary's case, if her images of the crucifixion had suggested that she was becoming self-absorbed and overwhelmed by her pain, the director might have tried to find an alternative image that would lead toward hope and strength. To suggest an alternative image can sometimes have the effect of diminishing the power of the negative image and attitude it embodies.

This attention to a person's use of images and symbols is a rather delicate one involving both an interpretive process which seeks to understand what a particular symbol means uniquely for this person and discrimination between images that may help or harm a person's spiritual development. One way of making this discrimination is to allow an image or symbol to play out its possibilities, making a judgment on the basis of its effects if it is allowed to continue to be a way of shaping thought, action, and feeling.[45]

In addition to "playing" out the possibilities in the images and symbols, it is also important to explore the personal meaning of some symbols in order to share in the directee's world of meaning and association with a symbol. Even symbols that appear to be archetypal, those which carry very similar meanings for most if not all people, become personalized.[46] Each person associates his or her unique life experiences with a given symbol. For instance, being submerged in water has different associations for a person who has nearly drowned than it has for a proficient bodysurfer.[47]

The way people in the direction situation express themselves through symbols and images varies depending on the role of symbol and image in the actual religious experience of directees. People have a pattern of images and symbols unique to them through which they communicate experiences. Sensitive direction requires the director to invite sufficient elaboration of the significant key images or symbols to ensure the possibility of grasping their meanings.

This chapter began with a description of narrative. It

explored the relationships of narrative form to human experience through Crites' analysis. It established the appropriateness and some of the advantages of using narrative forms for expressing experience. Finally, it indicated the importance of the role of imagery in the spiritual direction conversation.

In the following chapter the focus is on further benefits of narrative activity for the directee and ways directors can respond to these narratives. Of special importance among the benefits is the narrative construction of identity. The life story through which all of us construct our identities is something of an extended "metaphor of the self."[48] And insofar as the people in direction narrate significant episodes from their life story, these key symbols of the self will emerge in the conversation.

5

Benefits of the
Directee's Narrative Activity

The directee enjoys a number of benefits from personal storytelling in spiritual direction. Foremost among them is the opportunity to narrate one's life story in the presence of a receptive and interactive listener. Even more profound than the sharing of individual experiences through narrative is the sense of personal continuity created and maintained through a narrative construction of identity. In spiritual direction a narrative emerges which encompasses the person's spiritual identity and which may also reveal harmony and conflict among the various stories incorporated into that narrative. The directee further benefits from continuing to tell a story until its significance and implications are adequately assimilated. His or her storytelling tends to establish an attitude toward God and others, to engender sensitivity to God's activity in the directee's life, and at times to precipitate a moral struggle calling for changes in life style or activity in response to these experiences.

Finally, the director's response to the narrative can enhance the directee's appropriation of his or her own story. The director can invite elaboration of a story, assist in interpreting it, and analyze some features of the narrative. As a result, the directee often more fully appreciates the richness and depth of his or her story. This chapter, then, treats the narrative construction of identity, the effects of narrative activity for the directee, and responses of the director to the directee's narrative.

Narrative Construction of Identity

An approach to spiritual direction which pays attention to the narratives produced in this process is necessarily concerned with the narrative form of personal identity. Both individuals and communities construct their identities in a narrative fashion. Literally, the identity of a self or a community is embedded in and sustained by the stories they tell themselves about who they are. It is the story which maintains a sense of continuity through time and which symbolically interprets the whole history of the self or the community through certain key events. This story becomes the mode for expressing perduring values and meanings.

Personal identity has to do with three interrelated factors: the persistence of the self through time, the kind of person one is becoming (one's character), and the hermeneutical process dependent on memory.[1] The construction of identity is an ongoing activity of consciousness which coherently holds together these three elements in some meaningful pattern.[2] Narrative provides a structure for this activity of consciousness by its ability to symbolically interpret the whole of a personal history through a few characteristic events. George Stroup perceptively discusses this relationship between narrative and personal identity.

> It is no accident that when they are asked to identify themselves most people recite a narrative or story. . . .
> Often these narratives are simple and brief and contain only basic data, such as date and place of birth, vocation, family, etc. But with only a little probing it quickly be-

> comes apparent that every person's identity narrative is
> far more subtle and complex than it first appears. In an
> individual's identity narrative, what we might refer to as a
> person's "autobiography," certain events are lifted out of
> that person's history and given primary importance for
> the interpretation and understanding of the whole. . . . A
> person's identity, therefore, is an interpretation of per-
> sonal history in which the meaning of the whole and
> hence the identity of the self is constructed on the founda-
> tion of a few basic events and the symbols and concepts
> used to interpret them.[3]

In spiritual direction, the director is concerned with discovering the person's spiritual identity, the sense of self that is
experienced and consequently interpreted as related to the
divine being. Consequently, the directee's worth and significance are derived from God's unconditional love for him or
her. He or she is invited to respond in freedom to this offer of
love. Since all other human beings are also loved by God in
the same way, there is necessarily a social dimension to this
spiritual identity which reverences the spiritual identity of
others.

The fact that a person's spiritual identity emerges in a
dialogical process with the divine being poses an interesting
question as to who actually authors the narrative. Psychoanalytic theories seem to agree that a narrative construction of
identity is performed by the ego. The ego inevitably creates an
inadequate story of the self since it is the nature and function
of the ego to repress some events in the story it constructs. A
person's inability to create a coherent narrative with a reason-
able degree of accuracy in accounting for actual personal history becomes a key symptom of serious mental dysfunction.[4]

On the other hand, C. G. Jung and his followers, such as
James Hillman, give less emphasis to the deformation of the
client's narrative than to the story the psyche tries to tell

through images and symptoms that contest the story the ego maintains.[5] The goal of this kind of therapy is to heal the person through a telling of stories that are not totally controlled by the ego. These stories can contribute to modifying attitudes and behaviors espoused by the ego.

While both of the above narratives may be told in the spiritual direction situation, the primary story for which the director listens is the one God is trying to tell in, through, and with the person seeking direction. Navone and Cooper assert that "human stories are implicitly coauthored with God and neighbor."[6] The story is being told by the organizing ego-consciousness of the person.[7]

Insofar as the person is in relationship with God, God's activity will break into the narrative in such a way that it causes some kind of disorganization, contradicts an absolute form of self-assertion of the ego, or emerges as some inexplicable and mysterious confusion. When these intrusions into the narrative are attended to over time, it may become possible for the director to assist the directee in piecing together a story of God and this person which is not exclusively the story of the ego. The person's ego encounters a reality which contests its dominance and its attitudes as much as, if not more so, than the psychoanalytic account of the unconscious.

Theologically, the Judaeo-Christian tradition asserts that human history is the location of God's activity. When an individual experiences God, this encounter necessarily is experienced within the person's life story (history). Unfortunately many people do not articulate their identity/life story narratives to themselves in any comprehensive way unless their lives are unusual.[8] In the spiritual tradition, beginning with Augustine, those who wrote autobiographies in the form of confessions or religious testimonies thought their experiences relevant to others or were encouraged by spiritual directors to write accounts of their spiritual lives to teach others what they had learned experientially about prayer or the God-human relationship.

This tendency to restrict public sharing to persons of exceptional talent or grace often results in a sense of inferiority about the significance of ordinary people. Contemporary experience for many is characterized by a general loss of the meaningfulness of individual human lives in the face of the destructiveness of world wars, the nuclear threat, rapid cultural change and the depersonalization of human beings in increasingly technological societies.[9] The Judaeo-Christian tradition asserts even in the face of this depersonalization that each human being has worth and significance by virtue of his or her graced relationship to a personal God. Pastoral workers are encouraging ordinary people to engage in some kind of "life story conversation" in order to enable them to discover the religious meaning of their lives. People tend not to "tell the story" of their lives unless there is an occasion which prompts the telling.[10] The narrative construction of identity is a hermeneutical process of interpreting and making sense of the whole of one's life to this moment by creating a meaningful configuration.[11] Without occasions for such "tellings," the life story narrative tends to remain fragmented in consciousness and functions implicitly in the person's activity. Consequently, many people view their lives as a series of individual events, more like a collection of snapshots than a coherent story.[12]

The experiential realization of being personally caught up in the mystery of relationship with the divine other does not and cannot happen all at once because of the inherent historicality of human experience. It is a gradual process vulnerable to obstacles, personal, cultural, and social. Personal obstacles are the psychological blockages, which may be rooted in one's characteristic style of relationship with others, that are transferred to the God-human relationship. Cultural and social obstacles exist in the form of alternative identity stories which do not account for the existence of spiritual identity or which are opposed to the emergence of the kind of freedom vis-à-vis a culture and social groups which the spiritually mature achieve.

If people do not become conscious of their "personal myth," the story/stories they are living, they may not perceive that in a pluralistic society such as ours, they may be trying to live conflicting stories simultaneously. In the spiritual direction context the director listens for the story which exercises compelling authority over the life of the person seeking direction. And if it is not the Christian story, he or she challenges the person to reconstruct a story on the basis of the story chosen to be normative in one's life.[13]

Just as the emergence and solidification of a person's spiritual identity can be impeded, so, too, it can be fostered and encouraged. Historically, spiritualities are cultural, religious systems which include strategies for overcoming these obstacles to spiritual development. The process of spiritual direction is one of the specific means traditionally and currently concerned with fostering "the hidden orientation or directedness towards Mystery that is present in the core of each person's being and that corresponds with his or her unique spiritual identity or calling."[14]

Spiritual direction as a narrative event offers a social opportunity for telling and interpreting stories of religious experience which as a set of stories are Christian identity narratives. People seeking direction narrate their lives in the light of their personal experience of God, their shared convictions with the larger community of faith, and their vision of the people they are becoming. The interpersonal setting of this narrative occasion lends social reality and significance to experiences which contemporary American culture privatizes. Privatization of religious experience and the spiritual identity which emerges from it discourages a social articulation of this alternative sense of reality and social action required as a response to these experiences. By providing such an arena for exploring these experiences through first of all recounting them, and then discussing them in the light of a shared community of faith, the person in direction is supported and encouraged in attending to this dimension of reality and in responding to it.

Effects of Narrative Activity

A narrative approach to spiritual direction does more than foster the emergence in narrative of a person's spiritual identity. A director who is sensitive to the narrative representation of experience recognizes that more than one telling is often required by the directee in order to express adequately a key experience and assimilate it into the life story narrative. Further, the directee's narrative activity produces the following effects: creating narratives establishes the person's pervasive attitude toward God and other people, enables the person to relive religiously significant experience with greater appreciation for God's activity in his or her life, engenders an ongoing sensitivity to God's activity, and frequently precipitates moral struggle in response to religiously significant experience. Finally, the director can enhance the directee's appropriation of life experience through elaboration, interpretation, or analysis of the directee's narrative.

Retelling Key Stories
Phenomenologically, people tend to tell and retell a single story numerous times. Why is this so? There are two major reasons. First, multiple tellings of an important story constitute attempts to express what happened and to explore its meaning for the narrator. Experiences which are complex in

significance do not yield their meaning in one narration. Second, experiences which challenge the directee's assumptions or previous construction of identity require the person to reconstruct the life story in the light of this new experience.

An example of a story that would be likely to go through several retellings is the following:

> Several years ago a group of computer salesmen from Milwaukee went to a regional sales convention in Chicago. They assured their wives that they would be home in plenty of time for dinner. But with one thing or another the meeting ran overtime so the men had to race to the station, tickets in hand. As they barraged through the terminal, one man (the one telling this story) inadvertently kicked over a table supporting a basket of apples. Without stopping they all reached the train and boarded it with a sigh of relief. All but one. He paused, got in touch with his feelings, and experienced a twinge of compunction for the boy whose applestand had been overturned. He waved goodbye to his companions and returned to the terminal. He was glad he did. The ten-year-old boy was blind.
>
> The salesman gathered up the apples and noticed that several of them were bruised. He reached into his wallet and said to the boy, "Here, please take this ten dollars for the damage we did. I hope it didn't spoil your day." As he started to walk away the bewildered boy called after him, "Are you Jesus?"
>
> He stopped in his tracks and wondered.[15]

If the computer salesman, whose story this is, were to tell it in the direction context, it would probably not be in the polished form of this third person narrative. This man would be struggling to articulate and account for an experience of mystery which required something of him. How he would tell this story to a spiritual director would probably focus on his feelings about the event. What prompted him to return to the terminal? How did the blind boy's question affect him? What is Christ-like in his life? How might he be running too fast in his life? In what sense is he blind? Multiple retellings of this story would be in order until the man could render the experience in all its complexity and richness. Retellings of such a story aim not so much at narrative artistry as at a satisfactory narrative interpretation of the experience. Minimally, this interpretation includes both what happened and what it means to the narrator from the perspective of the present.[16] The man might return to the story again and again until he is able to decide concretely what he needs to change in his life in order to live out the implications of this experience. Whenever someone touches the mystery of human existence and/or the mystery which is the source of one's very being, a facile, single narration of the experience does not suffice to render it in all of its richness.

Secondly, if the salesman allowed himself to assimilate the effects of this experience through his storytelling, he would then begin to live and tell his life story with a different emphasis. He might choose to reflect on his life and notice when and how he was running so fast that other people were hurt. Or he might notice other ways he was not acting like the kind of person he wished to become. This narrative reinterpretation of his former story in the light of an event which questions the "story" he has been living, i.e. "running too fast," allows him to view his past behavior in the light of the new experience. The new experience calls him to assess a story he might have named "The Front-Runner Salesman" and to rename, reinterpret that story as "The Christian Who Was Blind to What Really Matters." This incident seems to suggest that a change in his life story is in order and so requires an alteration of it if the man allows the experience to challenge him.[17] Another experience might not require a change in the life story, but would simply be incorporated into the story as one more important event similar to the others by which the person organizes his or her identity-narrative.

Effects of Narration for the Directee

In spiritual direction, people frequently tell stories about experiences which are religiously significant to the narrators. These stories either have to do directly with God or with other people and life experiences which are illumined by God's presence. Spiritual direction has as its aim fostering a sensitivity to this dimension of life experience through first of all receiving these kinds of stories. Three major effects, which are rooted in the nature of narrative, result from the directee's telling these stories.

First, in creating religiously significant narratives, the narrator reenters the feelings and events narrated in a way that is often more powerful than merely noting patterns or talking analytically about the experience. Storytelling recreates the experience for the narrator and the audience with emotional power. This reliving of the experience through the narrative affords an opportunity for the storyteller to appreciate the experience more fully and to reenter the presence of the mysterious other originally encountered in the experience. For instance, each time the salesman tells his story and repeats the boy's question, he finds himself emotionally addressed again by it.

Second, narrating the experience establishes the narrator's pervasive attitudes and outlooks concerning either God or life lived in relationship to God. The way the story is told conveys the attitudes through the words which carry emotion and tone. The outlook is sometimes crystallized in a pithy sentence in which the narrator adds to the story what he or she got out of it. These attitudes and outlooks emerge from the narrative process itself and may or may not match the attitudes and outlook the person had during the experience. For instance, in the case study, Sam described an experience of call as "having lost it." These words carried his subsequent attitude of embarrassment more accurately than his original feeling of awe and love. If he had continued to tell this story emphasizing the embarrassment, this is the pervasive attitude he would have been establishing for himself as response to this experience.

Emerging from the first two effects is a third. Reliving the experience and establishing one's attitude and outlook "engenders a particular sensitivity and precipitates certain moral conflicts."[18] The computer salesman's story made him aware of behavior in his life to which he had been oblivious. He was sensitive enough to his own feelings when he got on the train that he was aware that something wasn't quite right. When he responded to that feeling by returning to the terminal, the subsequent events provoked further awareness and demands.

When he tells and retells this story, his increased sensitivity to the invitation to become more Christlike in his behavior is kept alive and operative in his heart and imagination. He is reinforced in his initial moral response to make restitution for the damage he had caused, and a new moral struggle is precipitated by the demand the story makes on him to change his behavior further. Telling the story thus keeps the tension of this demand present to his consciousness as he seeks to live out the meaning which the experience revealed.

These three effects, reliving the experience, establishing attitudes and viewpoint, and fostering sensitivity and moral struggle, flow from the activity of telling and retelling such a story quite apart from a response by an audience. The person explores the experience and its meaning by narrating it and continues to tell and retell it as a way of appropriating it into the life story and acting on its significance. Many of these tellings may occur in situations in which the audience is fairly passive. Each telling tries out a way of expressing the experience and its meaning for the narrator. Some audiences could, however, contest this meaning. For instance, the other salesmen, feeling a twinge of guilt, might not particularly want to hear about the blind boy and could even ridicule the man for going back to the terminal. Other people might deny the religious significance of the story and dismiss it as pure coincidence. These kinds of responses would affect how he tells his story in the future as he ponders its meaning for him and could even discourage him from continuing to tell it. Spiritual direction is especially concerned with religiously significant experience and affords what many people describe as a privileged opportunity for rendering these experiences into a narrative that can be received with reverence and sensitivity.

The Director's Response

As audience to a directee's narrative, the director can respond in a number of ways. Obviously, the first and most crucial response is that of attentive listening. The willingness to listen to others articulate the religious dimension of their experience is a *sine qua non* for all of the above effects on the narrator to occur at all. The spiritual direction situation is, however, characteristically interactive; the director is rarely only a passive auditor of the narrative.

In a narrative approach to direction, the director usually responds to the directee's story in narrative categories which respect the actual narrative as well as utilizing theological, psychological, and spiritual frames of reference. If my analysis of narrative is correct, these other frames of reference can be discovered within the narrative itself and could be used as ways of thematizing the particular experiences related in the story. Following the narrative clues, the director responds by eliciting further elaboration of narrative detail or additional narratives, by analyzing and commenting on the plot, tone of voice, image patterns, affects, conflicts, atmosphere, or character development, and by interpreting this narrative in relationship to the religious and cultural traditions. This attention to narrative clues allows the director to offer a non-judgmental response to the narrative because it focuses on what is "there" in the narrative. The director's response highlights or brings forward different facets of the narrative and explores their implications with the directee.

Spiritual direction is not "motiveless" in its intent. Its aim is to encourage the directee to recognize and respond to the spiritual direction God is unfolding for this person in the unique circumstances of his or her life. Accomplishing this goal presupposes in the director experiential and general knowledge of the spiritual life and a consequent prudential ability to co-discern with another the person's spiritual orientation. Ignatius of Loyola's "Rules for the Discernment of Spirits" portray two different types of people: some are basically oriented toward an increasingly God-filled life which they demonstrate by the overall quality of their lives and the effects of their activity; others are dominated by a tendency which leads away from God and the effects of their activity are manifestly destructive for themselves and others.[19] In addition to this general orientation, people also discover they can be mistaken about experiences which seem to promise to go in a certain direction but in actuality fail to do so. Discernment also, then, involves assessing how specific actions or events are related to an individual's general direction.

This intention to foster an orientation toward the good and God guides the director's response to narratives offered in spiritual direction. The director listens for narrative details that indicate whether the person is generally maturing or regressing in relationship to God. The director responds in a way that enables the directee to assess the progressive or regressive effect of particular experiences or choices upon his or her relationship with God. As the directee narrates various events of religious significance, the director's response to that narrative can enable the directee to grow in the self-knowledge which is one of the fundamental conditions for maturing in the spiritual life.[20]

Listening

The director can facilitate the directee's self-knowledge and growing God-awareness by listening in a way which welcomes his or her effort to tell a story that may be difficult to articulate. Frequently, experience of God is mediated through ordinary events and so is often a quite subtle background or almost hidden presence, which is nonetheless felt. The subtlety of such experiences makes them very difficult to describe. People value these experiences and frequently will not risk exposing them to ridicule or hostility because articulating them is difficult. The ability of a director to be fully present to the story of another and to encourage exploration of his or her experience may often be all the directee needs to concretize the experience sufficiently through narrative to receive it more fully.

The ability of a director to listen in this enabling way is often related to the quality of the director's own religious experience. The director usually needs to be receptive to the movement of God in her or his own life in order to be receptive to the mystery of God's interaction with others. In this kind of interchange between a directee who is telling a valued part of experience within the horizon of faith and a director who may be very silent, the directee may learn to listen to the story he or she is telling and to perceive what God is doing and how he or she is responding.

The enabling effect of reverent and attentive listening upon the narrator is due to the oral nature of this kind of narrative discourse. Few people persist in telling a story they sense is boring or disturbing to the audience. Storytelling as an oral event is strongly affected by the immediacy of the relationship which exists between the teller and the listener. A bond forms between the narrator and the audience which is its own form of intimacy.[21]

Eliciting the "Unsaid"

Second, the director may respond by inviting the directee to elaborate the narrative. Elaboration may be required in order to clarify both something in the sequence of the narrative and something about its meaning for the narrator. For instance, in the case of the sister on retreat, the director's eliciting a narrative about the details of her relationship with the priest and the immediate before and after of her prayer experience clarified that fantasies about her friend were not what caused her sexual feelings. The elaborated narrative further indicated that the feelings which emerged from the prayer experience lead to reverie about the friendship. In this same instance, in order to understand the relationship between the prayer experience and the friendship, the director invited a narrative about the friendship. Often a directee will respond to a question about the meaning of an event by telling another story about an experience that occurred at some other time in his or her life. The directee realizes that the director cannot understand what the present event means without being told how this event is either like or unlike some other part of the person's life story. Thus, the directee interprets the present story in part by offering another story.

In addition to inviting elaboration or expansion of meaning through another narrative, the director may also elicit that which lies "unsaid" by the narrator. According to Heidegger, it is of the very nature of articulating the truth that there is always something unsaid, something which could not be said at the time which later can be brought forward. The same case illustrates this principle as well. The sister could not describe her sexual feelings as an accompaniment of her experience of God, part of her response to God's interaction with her, because she thought these two things were incompatible. When the director mentioned some classical and contemporary writers in the spiritual tradition who had described and treated the relationship between the erotic and the spiritual, the sister could then create a new narrative which more accurately accounted for her experience.

Not only is there an "unsaid" which cannot be articulated because of conceptual difficulties or the lack of suitable categories, there is an "unsaid" that is a part of any imaginative construction. Ray Hart says:

> For everything said, there is a particular unsaid that is essential to imaginative meaning, an unsaid that is not stipulated but rather is iconically signified. For the immediately present, denotated, delineated actuality . . . there is a mediate, connotated, marginal background; iconic penumbrity is essential to imaginative meaning and reference. For every object grasped in imaginative symbol, there is a "world" in which self and object are disclosed to each other in polysemous intercourse.[22]

Gestalt therapy originated by Frederick Perls utilizes this principle as a major assumption in its work. For everything that is in the foreground which is fully articulated there is an assumed background. If someone uses the metaphor of a sandy beach, the ocean or lake lies in the background and is connoted by the beach in the foreground. A part that is brought forward implies the context of the whole that lies in the background.[23] Although a spiritual director may differ much from Fritz Perls in working with this background material, a director who is attuned to narrative clues will sense and invite the "unsaid" into explicit awareness. This "unsaid" is not something the director knows and of which the directee is ignorant. Rather, the director assists the directee in articulating what, at some level, the directee already knows and can articulate when it is elicited.

Finally, what is said in an oblique way can often simply go unnoticed in the direction conversation. Frank Kermode labels this quality in a narrative its "secrets." He argues that within the narrative itself there are clues or secrets which are at odds with sequence. These secrets in some way contest the narrative coherence achieved by sequence and if attended to could be significant.[24] In spiritual direction, the director may well need to invite elaboration of this kind of "story within a story." Experiences which the directee finds difficult to talk about and yet wants to express may only be hinted at in the narrative. If the director ignores these secondary clues, the directee is not likely to narrate this particular story as a main episode. In Sam's case, this narrative indirection or telling a story in "code" is operative in the description of his response to the ordination service as having "lost it." The director's positive acceptance of emotion combined with an expressed interest in the mysterious experience and Sam's estimate of it invited the elaboration of the more significant story partially hidden in the initial narrative.

Analyzing and Commenting on Narrative Elements

In a third kind of response to the directee's narrative, the director analyzes and/or comments on elements within the narrative primarily utilizing the vocabulary of literary criticism. This commentary may do any of the following: identify the plot pattern and possible outcomes, reflect back to the directee patterns of imagery, affects, themes, motifs, tone, and atmosphere, suggest alternative plots and/or related images, and identify conflicts among various sub-plots. All of these responses are based on narrative clues provided by the directee. Frequently, comments that help the directee notice what he or she has woven into the narrative enhance the directee's freedom of choice either to maintain this story and its direction or to change some part of it. Because these responses are respectful of the directee's freedom and honor the narrative, they tend to be received as non-intrusive and non-judgmental by the directee.

The director gives major attention to analysis of the plot since the plot embodies the directee's operative theories and provides a basis for predicting possible patterns of future action. Thus the director may abstract the pattern of the plot by renaming it according to an archetypal myth or fairytale, identifying it as comedy, tragedy, romance, satire, or comparing it to any other plot pattern available in the culture, i.e. "soap operas," "the Horatio Alger" story, etc. This analysis of plot structure may take one of several forms. Often simply restating the pattern in more general terms than the original story helps the narrator see his or her story as one particular instance of a typical pattern. Often the current major plot is repeated in one form or another in several sessions with different characters and scenes. Identifying this kind of plot helps the narrator recognize how he or she is typically organizing and interpreting experience.

An example comes to mind from experience in spiritual direction. One such pattern seemed to organize several episodes of one woman's narrative. She consistently related stories about herself in which she was somehow being victimized by others' demands or felt powerless. At the same time, in other scenes she exhibited a considerable amount of personal power. The director's describing for her the pattern of this repeating story and identifying the powerlessness/power motif helped her to make a connection between these conflicting plots and begin to resolve the difficulty.

Further, this particular story exemplifies how a person may be living two conflicting plots simultaneously. As a woman, she had internalized much of the cultural story of female powerlessness and actually perceived herself in that way. However, she also had developed considerable personal power which she wanted to exercise without taking responsibility for the use of that power. An exploration of these conflicting attitudes toward power and the way she was expressing them in her life story allowed her to recognize what she was doing and begin to adopt a different story.

To follow a story is also to recognize causal relationships of one event or attitude to subsequent ones. Once a story begins to unfold, the listener/reader wants to know not only what happened next but also where it is going. The listener/reader begins to project possible outcomes or consequences suggested by plot development as the story unfolds. Although the listener's projections may not be borne out as the story continues, sharing these projections with the directee may increase the options the directee has in concluding this particular episode.[25] Although some expectations about outcome may be suggested, both the director and the directee may be surprised by unpredictable events (complications) that intervene and shift the entire direction in which the story moves.[26]

Images as well as plot sequence indicate directionality. Mary's experiences are full of such images which could have been responded to at this level. For instance, three different times in her narrative she describes a torn and/or scarred face. Initially, she identifies with the Christ mask being torn to pieces in the paraliturgy. Her face, her identity and beauty, are being disfigured. She recognizes her story in Christ's suffering.

That enables her to choose to pray with an image of the crucifixion. Through her painful feelings she entered into the Christ mystery. In a subsequent interview, she elaborated: ". . . it was as if Jesus and I were one person and I began to realize that he experienced exactly the same thing that I did. It was really as if we were one person and I would use that and pray with it. And somehow I got this insight that he knew what it was like. It was very physical pain and that sort of sense that he was with that too. So I guess the images would merge almost."[27] This identification with Jesus resulted in intimacy, support and comfort. She described being understood, "and much more the hope that it would work out." Some form of resurrection/resolution was implicit in the pain through the images.

The third time, the image of the face emerged in a dream following the experience of God in the garden. "A young shallow girl with a flawless face had been replaced by a scarred, wrinkled woman." She describes the true beauty and love in the woman's face which parallels a similar quality in the crucified Christ. Mary is learning wisdom and love through her suffering. Her feminine images mirror the Christ images.

Her dream and prayer images presage the direction of healing and spiritual growth for Mary. Through a unique form of female suffering, rejection by her husband, she enters into unitive experiences with Christ crucified and God as lover. Simultaneously, feminine images of God—the wise woman and the friend who bandages the nearly severed head —begin to emerge. Both image complexes indicate the direction of Mary's growth and a subsequent revelation of the feminine in God. In a sense the images demonstrate a dynamic of positive resolution to Mary's suffering even while she is still feeling emotionally overwhelmed by her experience. To have pointed out to her this dynamic already present in her consciousness could have been extremely supportive to her.[28]

Each element of the narrative can be reflected back to the narrator as the director responds to it. Response to every element in a narrative would in all probability be too analytical. In a given narrative one or another element will seem to have greater emphasis. Sometimes, rather than working with the images, the director may redescribe the feelings evoked by the use of language or the general tone of the narrative, another time the plot; and still another time the director will focus on the atmosphere which permeates the narrative.

Atmosphere is an element in narrative that rarely receives attention in literary criticism. Wesley Kort defines atmosphere as "an image within a narrative of possibilities and powers which lie beyond the borders of human alteration, understanding, and control. . . . What lies beyond understanding and control is the common ground between religion and narrative."[29] Atmosphere is the element which allows the experience of "mystery" to enter into the narrative. These experiences of mystery result from the conditions of life, experiences both of limit and of otherness. A more extensive discussion of narrated experiences of mystery and its importance in spiritual direction narratives will be taken up in Chapter Six.

Relating the Narrative to the Tradition

In a fourth type of response to the directee's narrative, the director may explore the relationship between the story and the faith tradition in which it is rooted. This may be done by comparing the directee's narrative with other stories in the tradition, stories either in scripture or in the lives of saintly people. If the story seems to be a contemporary version of the Christian story which many other people also seem to be telling, the director may expand the directee's sense of belonging to a community by making that connection. The director may also respond to the story by suggesting or eliciting a connection between a particular narrative and theological categories such as providence, salvation, call, community, forgiveness, grace, etc. And finally the director may respond by suggesting the directee read or pray over a story from the tradition or contemporary community of faith related to the narrative.

Again, Mary's retreat is a case in point. Mary's psychological condition at the beginning of the retreat when she is locked in her house and afraid to let anyone in parallels the scene in the upper room on Easter night. When I mentioned this to Mary later, she responded very strongly to the suggestion. "I think probably, if I had had that passage, I would have realized that Jesus was already there and that would have been easier. I remember trying to open windows at home, and it was very hard for me to do that. So, yes, if I had had that image of Jesus having been in there, it would have been very helpful."[30] Likewise, when I asked Mary what scripture was like the experience she described as "an exchange of love that took me beyond control. I felt as if I were in a mystical garden,"[31] she immediately responded with the Song of Songs. Pointing her to that text or those themes in response to her description may have helped her stay in that loving embrace and feel there was some precedent in the tradition for what she was experiencing.

A spiritual director's ability to relate an experience narrated by the directee to the tradition may be one of the most crucial services the director renders to the directee. A competent spiritual director acquires this ability through his or her knowledge of the tradition and knowledge from one's personal history. This conscious awareness of the tradition and one's personal experience interpreted in the light of the tradition supplies the director both with some tried and true categories for dealing with experiences and the capacity to see things from multiple perspectives. Knowledge of the tradition opens this possibility because the tradition has, according to Gadamer, a rich and inherently contradictory character. The richness of the tradition and the conflicts within it generate in a person not a set of fixed categories but the ability to raise intelligent questions.

When a spiritual director can recognize in a directee's narrated experience something of the "variety of voices in which the echo of the past is heard,"[32] he or she is able to help the directee see the experience anew in the light of a whole host of stories or prior events. The ability to draw categories and frames of reference from the tradition serves to relativize the cultural concerns which in part constitute our contemporary "prejudices." These unconsciously determine the interpretive horizon in which the directee's experience is explored.

One of the problems of the Catholic tradition as it was transmitted through the late nineteenth century up to Vatican II was the sense that the tradition carried a set of fixed answers instead of multiple ways of raising questions and responding to them with various alternatives. The historical survey of the models of spiritual direction in Chapter One suggests something of the richness and conflicting variety in the tradition on this topic.

Experiences of God which are subtle and seemingly indescribable are historically conditioned even though they may appear to be atemporal. The tradition shapes both a person's understanding of these experiences and provides a vocabulary for expressing them. A primary vocabulary derives from scripture, both its narratives and its poetry. Another vocabulary is supplied by the mystics. A third vocabulary is developing in psychological language and practice which tends to interpret these experiences in an ahistorical way without reference to religious traditions. If spiritual directors are not able to connect their directees to the tradition which precedes contemporary psychology, the directees are deprived of the opportunity to experience a continuity of personal history with the larger tradition which actually is implicitly shaping their experience.

In all of the responses a director might make to the directee's narrative, the director profoundly respects the narrative on its own terms. This response to actual narratives occurs, first of all, by listening. Secondly, it ensures that elaboration, analysis, and interpretation originate from concrete events, images, and details in the actual narrative in order to assist the directee's self-understanding and perception of God's interaction with the directee in the context of the whole of life.

This chapter identified numerous benefits for the directee from telling his or her story in spiritual direction. A primary benefit is support for the directee's narrative construction of personal and spiritual identity. A second important benefit is the opportunity that spiritual direction provides for a directee to narrate religiously significant experiences until they are appropriated and the directee is satisfied with his or her response to their implications. Finally, the chapter elaborated a variety of ways the director can respond to the narratives offered by the directee. These responses include: listening, eliciting narrative detail or additional narratives, commenting on and interpreting narratives in literary categories, and relating these narratives to the tradition.

6

The Story Told by
the Person Seeking Direction

T he narratives produced in spiritual direction have several predictable and identifiable features. The primary subject matter of spiritual direction narratives is the directee's story of faith. The articulation of this story may either be explicit and direct or simply be the implicit background for the exploration of other issues in the directee's life. Regardless of what happens in any given narrative segment, it is the story of faith which provides the horizon within which all other narrative activity occurs.

The literary characteristics of spiritual direction narratives can be further specified as an oral form of life story, narrated in the temporal present by the directee, in a serial fashion, and in an interactive process. This life story is always unfinished, *in medias res,* selectively moving from the present to key episodes in the past and back to the present. Because of the serial nature of these narratives produced in periodic segments, it is an acceptable convention that new characters or events may be introduced in subsequent sessions without resolving unfinished plot lines from previous sessions. Finally, although spiritual direction narratives have an affinity with other forms of life story, namely biography, autobiography, and spiritual autobiography, the narrative situation causes spiritual direction stories to differ significantly from these other forms.

The Narrative Situation

The narrative situation of spiritual direction is ordinarily a one-to-one conversation between two people conducted within an intimate setting. As Chapter Three established, both persons share the horizon of a common spiritual tradition and can be characterized as living within the larger story of Jesus and the community of his disciples. In addition, spiritual direction is a social influence process in which the person seeking direction is willing to be influenced by the director who agrees to a regular series of encounters for the purpose of the directee's growth in the Christian life.[1] Because of the interactive nature of this process, the director is an interlocutor who responds to the narrative and elicits further reflection and narration by his or her response. These factors in the narrative situation of spiritual direction affect the telling of the story.

According to counseling theory, a psychological process transpires between the two persons in a helping relationship. Carolyn Gratton describes how the counselor "co-constitutes" the other: "It is after all, the counselor's unique personal perspective on reality, her relatively open or closed, broad or narrow, rigid or flexible perception of persons, events, and things that is the origin of her effective presence to the other."[2]

An important element in this vision of reality is the implicit view of what it means to be a human person. For the spiritual director this entails a conscious awareness of one's psychological theories of human experience, social process theories, and one's explicitly religious view which perceives the other to be loved by God and making some response to the grace offered.

This vision of another as constituted by God's concern for that person is crucial to the spiritual direction process and allows quite diverse stories of God and the self to be told in one's presence. As Chapter Five established, the human person's deepest identity is rooted in the God-human relationship. If this is true, telling a story of God from the perspective of one's life experience may result in finding oneself in God. The converse may also be true. Telling a story of searching for the self may end in finding God in oneself. The director's vision of graced human reality would, in part, be responsible for encouraging the story of searching for the self to proceed far enough to discover experientially the transcendent dimension of the human self.[3]

This spiritual vision of the human person is one of the primary differences between counseling/psychotherapy and spiritual direction. Spiritual direction takes place within a horizon, shared by both participants, of the reality of God as the context in which human life finds its meaning. Therapy usually takes place within a horizon which brackets the God question regardless of the specific beliefs of the persons involved.

The effect of these horizons on the storytelling is quite powerful. With God as the horizon of all experience, the story elaborated is one of a life interacting with this mysterious horizon and interpreting these experiences within a shared religious tradition. The spiritual direction story is a "story of faith" rather than a "story of Oedipal conflicts and their resolutions" as is told in a Freudian psychoanalytical conversation,[4] or the "story of individuation" in the Jungian framework, or the "story of development" as told from an Eriksonian perspective. What I wish to assert here is that the main plot is the "story of faith" although other interpretive paradigms and stories of human experience may appear as subplots. In Sam's case, his experience of psychoanalysis became one of the subplots in his spiritual direction narrative. He tended to encompass his story of therapy as one of the ways God was freeing him to be more whole. The healing that came through the therapeutic process was consciously experienced as grace. Even though he experienced intense emotional pain, he felt himself to be sustained and accompanied by God. His attraction to Jesus in his agony in the garden was one concrete manifestation of this graced interpretation of his therapeutic story. In another narrative situation, such as therapy, a story of faith may appear as a subplot but is rarely allowed to be the primary story.[5]

The climate created by the director's faith perspective and an expansive hospitality encourage the directee's attempts to articulate his or her spiritual identity and unique religious experience. In other words, psychologically, the spiritual perspective of the director is a facilitating factor in "co-constituting" the religious dimension of the person seeking direction. Secondly, the fact that both director and directee explicitly share a common faith horizon makes this conscious horizon of understanding the context for all of the narrative activity which takes place within it.

The Life Story

The story told in direction is an oral version of spiritual autobiography. Directees gradually construct a spiritual identity narrative when they tell a story of God in and through their own life stories. What are the literary characteristics of this kind of story?

As in autobiography, it is a first-person narration. The person seeking direction tells his or her own story assuming the role of both subject and narrator. The lapse of time between experiencing the events and narrating them creates enough distance to "allow for all the potentially ironical divergence in point-of-view between character and narrator that a novelist could require."[6] Thus, the directee narrates himself or herself as the major character, the hero or heroine, in the story. As narrator, the directee already gains some distance from the events narrated through his or her interpretive act of telling the story and begins to gain some objectivity.

Spiritual direction conversations facilitate a continual process of reinterpretation of the directee's past from the perspective of present experience. Like all autobiography, the story is narrated in the temporal present. The person's life prior to this spiritual direction relationship is encompassed by the current meaning and pattern the directee gives to his or her life. Significant "new experience," according to Gadamer, confounds expectations. Thus "new experience" provides a novel perspective which must be encompassed in one's self-presentation. In describing autobiography, Barrett J. Mandel says: "Autobiography forges present meaning into the marrow of one's remembered life."[7]

In spiritual direction, the directee does convey this present sense of his or her life and its meaning. However, unlike an autobiography the spiritual direction life story is not necessarily narrated from the vantage point of some important achievement. Rather, directees are compelled to fashion their life stories from the ordinary events of their present experience. For the director, beginning a series of spiritual direction conversations is an embodiment of the narrative convention, *in medias res.* Many details that would ordinarily be presented toward the beginning of a normal autobiography, especially episodes and significant material from the past, tend to emerge only in the form of "flashbacks" when something in the present experience evokes specific memory of the past. The near past and present experience of the person forms the temporal focus of the narration. The directee narrates events from the more distant past only when he or she assesses that they are needed by the director or when the present experience is directly connected to the past.

In Sam's case, this temporal feature can easily be seen although he omitted his accounts of past experience from the case. His initial self-presentation was restricted to his major issues in spiritual direction and the events occurring during the prior academic year. His only reference to the more distant past was the fact that he was an adult child of an alcoholic father. It was only later, when Sam wanted me to understand what he was experiencing in therapy that he would occasionally narrate paradigmatic episodes from childhood that illustrated the point he was making. For instance, in March he portrayed his father's characteristic manner of relating to him by describing how his father reacted to Sam's graduation from high school. Mary's case is even clearer. Her recently failed marriage is the event which challenges her sense of herself and which clearly places her retreat in the present moment constituted by this event. Her director gently reminds her of episodes she related to him earlier to help her find some point of contact between her earlier story and her present one.

Spiritual direction narratives require a level of self-disclosure that surpasses the restraints of formal autobiography. As is clear from the history of spiritual direction surveyed in Chapter One, spiritual direction requires the disclosure of the directee's motivation, temptations, confusions, ambiguities, painful and pleasant psychological and spiritual experiences. During eras when spiritual direction occurred in the context of sacramental confession, the directee's self-disclosure included actual sinful behavior. This material is normally excluded from public autobiography.[8]

This degree of self-disclosure is possible because the director plays the role of a trusted intimate. This sense of privacy and even more importantly trust in the confidentiality of the narrative situation supports the directee's tentative efforts to express himself or herself non-defensively in the narrative process. In a fruitful relationship, the directee presumes that the director is a friendly ally who does not ordinarily need to be persuaded to respond favorably to the directee. This attitude contrasts sharply with the strong rhetorical emphasis in the *memoirs* or *apologia* in which a life story is written precisely in order to defend the author against a public attack or an alternative perception of events.

Self-knowledge and insight about the directee's situation is one of the purposes of the narration. This insight occurs precisely as a result of the directee's freedom to discover his or her desires, motives, and actions through a narrative performance in interaction with the director. Because of the privacy and spontaneity of the narrative situation, spiritual direction life stories tend to be less self-consciously organized around pre-selected patterns than formal autobiographies. These more highly patterned stories require the omission of experiences or events which do not clearly fit the design. By contrast, spiritual direction narratives tend to include these kinds of experiences because they are the ones which have not yet been fully assimilated into the life story.

The major similarities and differences between spiritual direction narratives and other forms of autobiography have been established. Spiritual direction narratives are oral, spontaneous constructions from the vantage point of the temporal present. They are produced for a private, specific auditor, require greater self-disclosure, and tend to be less selectively organized than are autobiographies.

Since spiritual direction life stories do not unfold in a strictly chronological order, it remains to further specify the typical narrative pattern of these life stories and significant differences in the narratives told by men and women.

Pattern and Selectivity

As the case studies demonstrate, a spiritual direction narrative begins with the first direction appointment. Ordinarily, the directee begins the narrative by telling the director about his or her life. The purpose of this first interview is usually exploratory. In an initial telling of his or her story, the directee attempts to find out if he or she feels sufficiently comfortable with this person to continue and whether or not the director will be helpful. The director usually helps the directee disclose enough of his or her background and current situation for the director to sense if this is a person with whom he or she can work. Because of the exploratory nature of this conversation, directees vary considerably in the depth of self-disclosure they will risk until trust is established.

Sam's initial interview represents a high level of self-disclosure and a personality style which required no longer than halfway through the conversation for him to take some risk. I was surprised at how much he told me in the first session, especially the issues around which he was very vulnerable. I elicited his description about his usual prayer modes. Because I already knew Sam socially, he could presume I knew his more general background as well as the local context which we shared. Because he disclosed several emotionally charged and important recent experiences in this first session, I waited for him to fill in the details of family and community history as our conversations continued over the year. This occurred gradually, characteristically in the "flashback" mode when he needed to interpret present experience in the light of his past history.

Mary's pattern of self-disclosure was extremely slow and cautious. She found it very difficult to articulate what was happening to her and the process of disclosure took several retreats. It is easy to understand why her director was cautious about inviting elaboration after earlier experiences of reluctance. Although writers on spiritual direction assert that directors need a thorough account of a person's history, in practice this seems to take place when the directee feels secure enough to narrate it.[9]

These expectations are based on the directors' concept of spiritual direction, their experience as directees, and their cumulative experience of directees. In my small interview sample, I found that directors usually described the general expectation that it was appropriate for a directee to choose to talk about anything that seemed relevant to the person's life of faith and experience of God. Unlike a therapeutic situation, spiritual direction need not be "problem oriented." In the contemporary model of spiritual direction, the conversation is also no longer "sin" oriented as was the case in the post-Tridentine model.

Because of its oral mode and the particular context, selectivity of detail is determined by the person's perception of the director, by the person's perception of what spiritual direction is, and by the present issues and emotional situation of the person. Because the person is shaping his or her story for a particular director, details are chosen in such a way as to locate common ground between the two people. The director does affect the directee's narrative by the quality of attention given to particular topics or issues. Interest may be demonstrated by the director's quality of presence, by the questions put to the directee, or by other interpretive comment. In my experience as a directee, I noticed that I would omit experiences which seemed to bore the director or which never received verbal comment. In addition to the actual responses of a director, literary critical theory suggests that the director receives the projections of the "implied audience" or "implied reader" created by the narrator.[10]

The narrator projects an image of what a spiritual director is interested in and shapes the narrative accordingly. In

Sam's case, the first half of his opening narrative had to be based on such a projection since he knew me in a very limited way. I think the director is given a variety of roles to play by this fictive projection. The director either chooses to respond according to the way the narrative marks out the role or breaks the projection by declining to accept some part of the projection by his or her actual responses.

Once a direction relationship has been initiated, the pattern of narration after the initial interview unfolds within the structure of a serial. The time intervening between sessions, each of which is its own discrete narrative unit, functions much the way beginning a new chapter in a novel allows the author to introduce new characters or leave a plot line unfinished temporarily.[11] In the spiritual direction conversation, the intervening time and the purpose of direction contribute to the acceptability of considerable discontinuity in the narrative.

An episodic structure results from this seriality. The narrative units which follow the initial interview are usually composed of separate episodes that have occurred since the last meeting. The time frame remains in the temporal present which is measured from the last conversation. Directees select the events which appear to be the most important from among the events they have experienced. In a sense, life does the selecting.[12] The directee's initial selection of both subjects and sequences of action (plots) already forms "a kind of plot" which represents some "tension" point seeking resolution. The directee begins to fashion connections among the events narrated through the narrative process itself. If Iser is correct, the "reader" in these narratives, the director, is as involved as the narrator in discovering the connections among the stories.

Directees frequently select subjects for narration from among the following experiences: an unresolved conflict or troublesome experience, the particular way they perceived

God to be interacting with them during prayer or through some other event, the effects of social reality, invitations to change or grow, relationships, or something related to work or ministry. Typically, these events may be "highs" or "lows" although people who are in a relatively problem-free period may tell a story of simple, ordinary, and subtle experiences of grace that tend to go unnoticed during more turbulent times.

Each incident chosen for narration may at first appear to be a distinct narrative unit with no apparent connection, either to others in the same conversation, or to the story told during the previous session. Occasionally these incidents seem to be related only because they occurred within the same two or three week period of time. However, each of these incidents is set off against preceding segments. Gradually, a story builds because of the reciprocal relationships among the narrative elements.[13]

Stylistically, these units might be described as *cinéma verité* excerpts.[14] Gradually, both the directee and the director begin to construct coherency and connections among the disparate stories told. The protagonist of each episode may or may not be the directee. However, one unity of narration resides in the narrative voice, the "I" who provides a consistent narrative perspective in each episode. From this continuous narrative voice, the character of the directee gradually unfolds. A second unity of narration gradually emerges in motifs and themes (the values and meanings espoused)[15] which are compelling for the narrator. And a third unity of narration emerges in a characteristic repetition of behaviors and attitudes on the part of the protagonist. This latter unifying element matches a novelistic interest in a "developing character" which provides an incipient plot structure for these sequential narrative units.[16]

There are also, however, discontinuities in the narration. Characteristically, there are many interwoven plots in the life story emerging linguistically in each session. A narrative sequence related in one session may or may not be resumed in the next session. The listener learns to avoid the curiosity which would ask "What happened next?" when the story was broken off at the end of the last session. The life may have moved to a new center of interest or another plot line although the tale has been left uncompleted for the listener. While the listener may refrain from directing the story line into the trajectory indicated by the last session, the listener does follow that theme when the narrator develops this particular plot line in a subsequent session. The director may need to elicit a return to a theme or plot line if she or he suspects there are unresolved or unfaced issues which dictate the broken-off plot line rather than merely an unfinished narration of already completed action. In direction the director needs to discriminate between an incomplete narration and the directee's inability to integrate some experiences into the narrated life.[17]

Some Differences Between Men's and Women's Narratives

In addition to the characteristic narrative features described above, there are significant differences in narrative style between men and women. Feminist literary critical studies of autobiography contrast a unidirectionality in men's lives with a multidimensionality in women's lives. Men's unidirectionality finds its narrative counterpart in a linear narrative in which they unify their stories by concentrating on one theme, period, or characteristic of their personalities. By contrast, women's lives, rooted in their flexible social roles, are more frequently characterized by a multidimensionality which creates a pattern of diffusion and diversity when they write. "The narratives of their lives are often not chronological and progressive, but disconnected, fragmentary, or organized into self-sustained units rather than connecting chapters."[18] Suzanne Juhasz makes this point even more concrete:

> When you ask a woman, "What happened?" you often get an answer in the style that McClelland has labeled circumstantial, complex, and contextual. . . . The woman is omitting no detail that she can remember, because all details have to do with her sense of the nature of "what happened." A man, on the other hand, will characteristically summarize: give you the gist, the result, the *point* of the event. In their form, women's lives tend to be like the stories that they tell. They show less a pattern of linear development towards some clear goal than one of repetitive, cumulative, cyclical structure.[19]

In spiritual direction, women tend to narrate their lives with a wealth of detail, affect, and imagery.[20] Their need to narrate their sense of the nature of what happened has often been negatively judged by directors operating from male standards who judge this wealth of detail as unnecessary or not to the point. What can fail to be appreciated is that the point for women is the story they are telling in its diffuse form of narration. This narrative style corresponds to the way women experience their lives. They characteristically attend to several types of experience simultaneously without necessarily unifying them in relationship to each other. Frequently, the opportunity to tell the story creates a unity of its own without achieving a unified plot in its first narration.

As a directee, I find the above description accurate. When I began to learn to tell my story in direction, I often felt I was giving more detail than the directors I was seeing probably found helpful. At the same time, I didn't see how they could help me if I did not completely convey to them what I was experiencing. When I condensed my narratives to summaries, I questioned my motives for selecting the omissions. If I left out what was confusing to me, then there was nothing with which I needed help. I felt I needed to account for the whole quality of my diverse experiences for the director to understand who I was. It was only after two years of regular direction that I could begin to discriminate what could be omitted although I continue to prefer sharing a sense of the multidimensionality of my life in a richly detailed narration.[21]

Men exhibit contrastive characteristics in their storytelling. Just as women are multidimensional in their narratives, men are unidimensional in theirs. They tend to control their narrative self-disclosure by limiting affective and descriptive detail. Typically, men emphasize actions or meanings. Even though Sam expresses his emotional experiences with greater facility than most of the other men I have seen in direction, he nevertheless reported his feelings of embarrassment during the session in which he agreed to visualize a feeling he could not yet name. One sentence in objective language can both conceal and reveal intense affective experiences. Men frequently require the invitation of a guide or friend to expand the description. The facilitation of the director/guide can help male directees to explore and become comfortable with the emotional qualities in their experience and then incorporate this story into their particular form of the male story without unnecessarily threatening their self-image.

Sam's case does demonstrate some aspects of male affectivity as it emerges in the narrative. Although Sam was usually aware of his feelings, he was not altogether comfortable with disclosing them. His describing his experience at the diaconal ordination as "having lost it" is a typical male rendition of an emotionally positive experience expressed first in a negative form. The negative judgment about loss of self-control reflects his male conditioning. Men do not cry in public, even in a liturgy. The first form his narrative took was reinforcing this conditioning. When pressed to be more concrete about what happened before "losing it," Sam described an interior, felt, sense of being called to ordination, lovable and acceptable to God just as he was. The invitation I offered him was to tell this part of the story as the main plot instead of focusing on the embarrassment over loss of emotional control—to tell the story of the love and acceptance rather than the secondary story of loss of emotional control in public. To retell the story in this way was to match the dominant affect with narrative form which allowed the depth of the experience to continue to be present in memory as well as in its emotional effect. Telling this story differently also has the effect of resisting the dictates of dominant, male, social norms, at least within the privacy of spiritual direction.

While I often find male "directness" in narrative style refreshing, the male tendency toward unidimensionality in storytelling can be a drawback. Men can feel they've told the whole thing with great economy of expression and in a highly unified pattern while they actually may have censored out the story more appropriate to spiritual direction.

The director's responses to the narratives related by men and women need to take into account their differences. With a women directee, the director can very helpfully extrapolate two or three major themes from a great quantity of narrational detail. Naming them for her may be revelatory and helpful since she may not yet have become explicitly conscious of them herself. Focusing on one episode and exploring it in depth can begin to allow her to see all of the story in a new light. With men, the challenge is often to elicit greater concrete detail and nuance in the feelings. The male directee is likely to censor out the story that feels too chaotic or confused to tell. He needs to be reassured that he can tell an experience which he can not yet easily incorporate into his narrative unity.

Telling Stories of the Experience of God

For many people seeking spiritual direction, learning to tell the story of their experience of God and of a life story lived within the larger story of Christian faith is the central task in spiritual direction. Experiences of God are among the most difficult to tell for many people. American culture since the 1960's permits people to describe and tell stories of peak experiences so long as they are secular in their interpretation and triggered by drugs, sex, or music. In the 1980's, the permitted religious narrative is a privatized version of a "born again" Christian fundamentalist story. However, stories of falling into the realm of a strangely loving mystery which subtly allures one and insists on response are not so easily told even in the direction situation. There are no cultural forms for these highly personal and unique encounters with the holy. Habits of language and social convention work against telling one another the deepest stories of life and meaning, especially if they are laden with strong affect. These might be experiences of being flooded with love and care, gentleness and acceptance, call and challenge. It seems that the story in our culture which initially requires being "told slant"[22] is the story that emerges from religious depths.

What characterizes experiences of God and the stories articulating them? Chapter Four discussed what is understood as experiences of God. Here, I want to expand that discussion with a more concrete description of the way these experiences are represented in narrative. Through these kinds of experience, one becomes aware of that which eludes comprehension and yet utterly transcends the human person. That which transcends us is given the name "mystery," or in Rahner's phrase "Holy Mystery,"[23] as a new naming of God. This mystery is sometimes experienced not simply as that which constantly eludes us or as the "term of human transcendence" but as a transcendence which comes toward us, breaking in upon our everyday existence in a mysterious way as gift. Edwards names this type of religious event an "experience of grace."[24]

Spiritual direction helps people identify and tell their personal experiences of such moments in their lives. It provides an opportunity to explore and express their own relationship with this holy mystery that may free them from inadequate/inaccurate images and concepts of God or the burden of "oughts" and "shoulds" about what a relationship with God entails. People often experience difficulty recognizing a similarity between their "churchy," conventional expectations of God and these more general, less religiously languaged experiences of God as the ground and horizon of their being.

These stories are pervaded by an atmosphere of mystery as a strange presence to live with when it intrudes into a person's life. The mood of the narration will be reverent, filled with awe, including its mixture of both attraction and fear. And the effect on the listener is a corresponding response of awe in receiving this story. Although fear of this strangely uncontrolled and uncontrollable reality may be present, there is often a more fundamental tone of joy and gratitude—a conviction of the significance of the reality present in this mode and its meaningfulness to the directee.

Only after a person is able first of all to honor these experiences of the mystery dimension of life and narrate them interiorly or in the context of spiritual direction does a person grasp with any degree of coherence the particular way God interacts with the person in and through his or her personality, history, relationships, level of psychological development, and activities. Learning to tell this story of grace enables the directee to grow in responsiveness to this experience. In traditional language, that is growth in faith, hope, and charity. The person's life becomes gradually more oriented toward God in all of its dimensions. The unique pattern and specific interactions of this person with God, who both encompasses the whole of the person's life and remains always beyond grasp, become conscious and engender response.

John Shea is very helpful in pointing out that contemporary culture makes it very difficult to receive these experiences of mystery. The technological spirit of the age fosters a manipulative, controlling, restricting attitude to the environment and other people. It does not cultivate a receptive, contemplative, or appreciative attitude.

> Although the technological spirit does not mean automatic insensitivity to Mystery, we do live in an age tempted to a secular restriction on consciousness. This temptation is often caricatured as the flat-earth impulse, the tendency to level all vertical awareness to a horizontal understanding. Anything that smacks of transcendence is immediately flattened.[25]

Because our awareness of mystery is not fostered by the culture, many people need help in identifying these experiences. There is a need to hear stories of encounters with mystery which might serve as contemporary narrative paradigms. There is especially a need for stories which take place in everyday life and which are not specifically contextualized in religious settings or restricted to a religious vocabulary.[26] Frequently, people's notion of experience of God may be too narrow to include experiences that happen outside of prayer. An example may illustrate these difficulties more clearly:

> A farmer who had agreed, reluctantly, to attend a workshop on Christian faith found himself confronted with the question: "Is there any special time in your life when you find yourself overwhelmed by a sense that there is some-

thing more than yourself involved, something more than
you can account for, a time when something seems like a
gift given from beyond yourself?" For the first time, in a
session lasting several hours, the farmer's face showed interest, and after a while he volunteered a comment: "I feel
like that sometimes in the early mornings when I am out
in the middle of a crop of wheat and I hold a grain of new
wheat in my hand." He went on to say that he had never
talked to anyone about this experience before, even
though it had happened over many years. The experience
had been so overwhelming as to be almost inexpressible,
and he had felt that others would not understand what he
was talking about. As the discussion continued it became
clear that, while the farmer went to church regularly, and
sometimes prayed, he had never, to this point, explicitly
connected his experience in his wheat crop with anything
in his Christian faith.[27]

Shea and Edwards specify a number of such occasions or
"triggers" which may initiate experiences of mystery if a person grasps this dimension of the experiences. Edwards uses
the broad categories of experiences of "richness and abundance" and those of "limit or vulnerability." Both of these
categories are potentially limitless, but some specification is
helpful. Among the experiences of richness and abundance
which surpass what can be attributed to the human participants are: interpersonal love, creativity, forgiveness, child-
birth, parenting, and beauty. Among the experiences of limit
are the following: vulnerability, death, failure, loneliness, and
alienation. These experiences of limit often disclose a depth
dimension or a loving presence that comes to one in and
through a painful or frightening situation. In each of these
experiences of limit, the situation evokes or changes into a
qualitatively different experience which becomes the experience of mystery. For instance, Nouwen's description of the

way loneliness may open into an unlonely experience of solitude indicates the possible nuances in such a change.[28]

In *Stories of Faith,* John Shea talks about revelatory encounters with mystery as an ordinary and unavoidable human process. He elaborates a structure of five elements in these experiences which are accessible to analysis although the people involved may never articulate these elements to themselves. The five elements as Shea describes them are:

> [1] There is a relationship to the Mystery of life. [2] This Mystery communicates meanings about the nature of the relationship. [3] This meaning is initially formulated and then pondered, acted on, rephrased, repondered, reacted on, etc. [4] The meaning that is received is related to the conflicts, questions and needs of the people involved. [5] Although there is an enshrined religious vocabulary to talk about the felt perception of these experiences, it is seldom used. This last element is a special characteristic of contemporary revelation-faith experiences.[29]

Shea aptly describes some of the narrative features of these stories and how people appropriate the meanings disclosed in the experiences. First of all, each of the experiences Shea describes finds its way into a narrational situation. A salesman tries to tell another something that "struck" him when he was with a friend they both knew. In another, a college girl is telling her family about what hearing Mother Teresa evoked in her. In a third, a man in his mid-forties is telling the rest of his family what he spontaneously said to his dying father. In each instance, the person who has encountered the mystery dimension of life is struggling to articulate something about the experience to another person.

Chapter Five discussed how people often tell such a story numerous times until they have adequately grasped and formulated the meaning of such an experience. Once the value or

truth has emerged through these tellings, a meaning emerges
that accompanies the person through life. The kind of truth
which emerges in these "faith formulations" may seem quite
arbitrary if it becomes severed from the concrete events which
generated it. It is important to keep in mind the provisional
kind of truth which arises in a life story.[30] Every such meaning
is liable to revision on the basis of a new experience of relationship with mystery.

Shea's fourth element addresses the relationship between
the meaning received from mystery and the particular questions, crises, situations of the person at the time of the experience. Thus the college girl interprets her response to mystery
in terms of commitment and the ideals that govern one's life
choices. Or the salesman, not far from retirement, interprets
his experience in terms of relationships with grandchildren.
And the man whose father died talks about "letting go" which
is appropriate to the surrender death is. In the case study, Sam
interprets his experience at the diaconal ordination and his
response to the song, "I Need You," in relationship to his
vocational commitment. Mary's identification with the
paschal mystery is clearly related to the pain of her divorce
and its aftermath.

Finally, Shea's last element, the language chosen to articulate these experiences, offers an important linguistic clue to
the secular vocabulary many contemporary people adopt for
religious experience. Shea argues that even in a culture which
does not adequately provide a specific vocabulary for these
experiences, nonetheless they are neither lost nor unex-
pressed. Rather, they are expressed in a "more subtle use of
secular language."[31] Shea gives the following examples of this
use of secular language: "That's what it's all about"; "Without
this it wouldn't be worth living"; "That's damnable"; "A life
without love is tragic"; "It's pathetic the way she is squander-

ing her youth." All of these expressions hint at a larger dimension in life. Further, Shea identifies another manner of speaking which talks not about the things of life but about "life" itself. He considers this focus on life a linguistic clue that the underlying experience has had the impact of revelation and been responded to in a faith mode.[32]

Several directors identified other linguistic clues which signal the narration of experiences with mystery in their practice of spiritual direction. When directees begin to tell these stories, some change occurs in the story. Either the story stops for a while and lapses into silence or language becomes more halting as people search for language.[33] Authentic religious experience usually requires a recourse to metaphorical expression which often has a fresh and unique character to it.

Narrative characteristics of these stories of mystery can be summarized as follows: they are about the directee's encounter with ultimate reality; they may be expressed in subtle uses of secular language; they require a metaphorical use of language; they often include a statement of the truth distilled from the experience; they convey an atmosphere of reverence or awe through lapses into silence and a struggle to find words.

Chapter Five already elaborated several effects of narrative activity on the directee. In relationship to articulating these stories of mystery, I want to describe one more effect. In the contemporary model of spiritual direction the directee is encouraged to tell whatever his or her experience of God is. Unlike the post-Tridentine model when confession of sin was the context for spiritual direction, the person seeking direction is not required to tell a story of sin and failure as the dominant theme of the story although directees do come to face their sinful tendencies and experiences. The contemporary model of spiritual direction encourages directees to tell a story of faith and God's involvement with them rather than restricting the narration to a story of sin and forgiveness. This theme emerges only as subplot within the larger story of grace and faith.

This chapter has identified the narrative patterns and literary characteristics of spiritual direction narratives. It has examined the temporal focus, the seriality of these stories, and the relationship of narrative units to one another. It proposed that the directee's story of faith is the horizon within which all the other life story narratives are told. Finally, it further specified features of stories of mystery and their effect on the directee. It remains to discuss in Chapter Seven the effects of the directee's narrative activity on the director.

7

Conclusion

By way of conclusion, I wish to make explicit some of the implications of this narrative analysis of spiritual direction for the director who participates in this ministry as well as to retrace the path of this argument as a whole.

The Effects of Narrative on the Director

In the process of spiritual direction, as previously asserted, the director is an active participant in the directee's storytelling. Participation in another's life story puts the director "at risk" if the director remains open to the truth of the directee's life and becomes involved in the story.

Because narrative discourse engages its auditors affectively, intellectually, and imaginatively, the director finds himself or herself involved with the directee's story. If the director is truly participating in the conversation as a partner in search of the truth of the directee's story, the director is engaged in such a way as to be addressed by the truth that emerges from this cooperative dialogue. According to Gadamer, that truth is valid for both people.[1]

The fact that the director's genuine engagement in the directee's story yields the possibility of a truth that belongs to both is a consequence of the reciprocity inherent in all "I-Thou" relationships. There is always a "fellowship" between two people in relationship. As Gadamer states: "The experience of the 'Thou' must be a specific one, in that the 'Thou' is not an object but is in relationship with us. . . ."[2]

Gadamer contrasts this kind of experience of another with one which

> . . . seeks to discover things that are typical in the behavior of one's fellow men and is able to make predictions concerning another person on the basis of experience. We call this a knowledge of human nature. We understand the other person in the same way that we understand any other typical event in our experiential field, i.e., he is predictable.[3]

This approach to another denies the reciprocity in the relationship. In this mode, the one who turns the other into some "typical" category removes himself or herself from the possibility of truly being addressed by the claims of the other.

Gadamer describes a third kind of experience of the "Thou" which removes one person from being addressed by the claims of the other. In this mode, the "Thou" is acknowledged as a person; but despite the involvement of the person seeking to understand, this understanding is a form of self-relatedness rather than other-relatedness.

> This relation is not immediate, but reflective. To every claim there is a counter-claim. That is why it is possible for each of the partners in the relationship reflectively to outdo the other. One claims to express the other's claim and even to understand the other better than he understands himself. In this way the "Thou" loses the immediacy with which it makes its claim. It is understood, but this means that it is anticipated and interpreted reflectively from the standpoint of the other person.[4]

This attempt of one partner in the conversation to remove oneself reflectively from the influence of the other person is detrimental to the spiritual direction relationship. In spiritual direction, the director wants to facilitate the directee's growth in his or her core spiritual identity as that person encounters God. If the director alters the direction relationship in an effort to dominate the other or resist the claims of the other person's life on the director, little that is fruitful for the directee can happen.[5]

The director is both a receiver in this mutual enterprise and "at risk" to be challenged by the directee's story. How does the director receive? First of all by participating in the directee's meaning-making process. The revelatory truth about life and relationship to the holy which emerges from the directee's religious experience can contribute to the director's own meaning-making process. If the meaning which emerged cooperatively in the conversation has validity, there must be some way that this truth emerges for the director in his or her particular situation as well as for the directee. One's directees become characters in the director's life story. Their willingness to disclose their spiritual identity, their lives as transformed and addressed by ultimate reality, encourages and challenges the director to live in relationship to the same ultimate reality.

Since the directee and director participate in the same faith tradition and stand together as brothers and sisters in faith, the directee's faith story can function as a contemporary proclamation of the "gospel" to the director. In spiritual direction, the relationship between director and directee differs remarkably from a therapeutic situation in which questions of values and beliefs are not presumed to be shared by the therapist and client. In spiritual direction, director and directee are both addressed by and stand within a common faith tradition. Insofar as the directee's life story genuinely embodies some concrete aspect of that faith tradition, the director is addressed by it and challenged to respond. For instance, in Sam's case, much of the year's direction focused on vocational discernment. He consistently experienced a felt sense of call and acceptance from God encouraging him to finalize his religious commitment in the context of Jesuit life and priesthood. What effect does this have on me, the director? Sam's generosity of response to his call invites me to a renewed fidelity to my religious commitments. Although, as a director, I would not necessarily discuss with Sam my response to God to whom I am drawn through Sam and his story, I am nonetheless affected. I can allow his story to address mine or I can resist its impact.

The director must have a capacity for genuine openness if he or she is to be affected by the claims that directees' life stories make:

> In human relations the important thing is, as we have seen, to experience the "Thou" truly as a "Thou," i.e. not to overlook his claim and to listen to what he has to say to us. To this end, openness is necessary. But this openness exists ultimately not only for the person to whom one listens, but rather anyone who listens remains fundamentally open. Without this kind of openness to one another there is no genuine human relationship. Belonging together always also means being able to listen to one another. When two people understand each other, this does not mean that one person "understands" the other, in the sense of surveying him. . . . Openness to the other, then, includes the acknowledgement that I must accept some things that are against myself, even though there is no one else who asks this of me.[6]

When this type of relationship exists in direction, the director finds that he or she is constantly learning from directees. By

welcoming the validity of the directee's experience, the director gradually grows in his or her capacity to exercise *phronesis*
as was discussed in Chapter Three. The director's experience
of life is expanded by learning through directees' experiences.
The director gains broad experience of a wide range of people.
Hearing many narratives about how good people actually resolve and respond to a variety of situations enlarges the range
of possible action for the director in his or her life. The director not only finds new ways he or she might conduct himself
or herself in a given situation but also modifies and adapts the
guiding ideal of the good person on the basis of what good
people actually do.

Being with directees is often a "sacramental" experience
in Shea's vocabulary. "In and through" the people the director sees for direction, the director experiences God acting and
alive in his or her world. The directee's sharing of faith experience through story can become a moment of communion in
the same reality disclosed by the story. In recounting stories of
faith, the directee, among other things, relives the experience
and witnesses to it. The director imaginatively participates in
this story and can at the same time experience, in and through
the directee, God actively present within the direction setting.
Paul Janowiak described this kind of experience when he
talked about the effect on him of being with one directee.

> Just yesterday, after I had finished with someone, I recog-
> nized that I was harried from the week when I began a
> direction session. During the session, this woman directee
> had been describing her feeling of being deeply graced
> during the week. She had been talking about Mary and
> waiting for Jesus to be born. When I was setting up the
> next appointment, I said to her: "I just want to tell you
> that every time you come and we have these sharings, I
> always end up feeling more whole."[7]

Secondly, the directee's story may elicit the director's memories of his or her religious history. Again, I can use Sam's case and his vocational discernment as an example. As Sam uniquely experiences the way God and his experiences indicate the appropriateness of his decision, I relive my own equally unique experiences which led me to my perpetual profession. His story, disclosing his pattern of grace, evokes both the similarities and the differences in my story. To a certain extent, we both share the same story because we both stand within a religious tradition which has historically maintained a particular, institutional style of religious living. However, the way we live that story differs because of gender and other personal differences. This shared tradition is the horizon within which we both interpret our experience of call and response.

When a directee presents the meaning derived from an experience, such as "All real life is meeting," the director may find that its formulation does not evoke immediate agreement. To resolve this dissonance, the director frequently traces the evolution of this "truth" from the concrete situation and the questions or conflicts confronting the directee at that moment. Frequently, these words of truth are not applicable to the director because his or her life situation differs from the directee's. According to Shea, "What happens in the revelation-faith experience is closely connected to what is happening in us before the experience. The needs that are troubling us, the drives that are urging us on, the conflicts we are engaged in shape the content of the revelation."[8] The meaning derived from a given experience by a directee may be limited in its validity to a specific time or circumstance. However, once the formula is traced back through the directee's story, the narrative may suggest a different meaning that addresses the director's situation.

This effect is rooted in the nature of narrative and the constructive act of the director/auditor. Narratives do not present only one possible meaning or truth. Rather, the complexity of perspectives provided by the plot, characters, narrator, and implied reader invites the auditor to construct his or her meaning for the narrative as it proceeds.[9] Different auditors/directors are liable to construct different, yet equally valid meanings from the narrative clues to which they give greater or lesser emphasis. Thus, directors are actively engaged in their process of constructing meaning from the interplay of these perspectives as they follow the story being told.

According to Iser, the reader actively projects possible scenarios in relationship to the "blanks" in the story. The seriality of direction narratives tends to increase the activity of the director in making connections between parts of the story that have not necessarily been connected by the narrator in the telling. The director needs to be aware that the connections he or she makes between themes, actions, and meanings may not be at all the same for the directee.

Just as directees become characters in the life story of the director, so too directors become characters in the directee's story. As a director, I have not gotten used to being a character in the stories of the people I see for direction. Sam's version of a year in spiritual direction is not necessarily the way I would have told it. As Roy Schafer says, "We narrate others as we narrate selves."[10] I have no control over the way directees narrate me in their stories to others, concretely how Sam narrated me in the case study. He telescoped an exchange which unfolded far more gradually than he recorded it. My notes on the ordination experience included the tone of his voice, its volume, its level of excitement which was incongruent with the words "I lost it." I first asked him, "Did it feel good?" Sam replied, "Oh, yes!" (with emphasis). I then asked him how it felt good and he proceeded to describe the feelings of love and acceptance from God he wrote in the case.

In addition to this more gradual process of drawing out the story, there were other observations about Sam's narrative rendering of this incident. Since Sam was living primarily in a male situation, we discussed the problem of how much to tell and what he could say in a positive way about this experience to other men who had seen him in tears. I helped him distinguish between what he said to other people and how he told his story to himself.

I doubt Sam would disagree with these additional details. If he wishes to portray me as more direct and challenging than I feel I am, that is nonetheless his perception and experience of me in direction. Or it could simply be another example of the differences in narratives created by men and women as discussed in Chapter Six.

In summary, the director is affected by the directee's narratives. The director remains (or ought to remain) consciously interactive and mutually participative in the spiritual direction conversation. If the conditions of a genuine conversation discussed in Chapter Three are operative, the director is addressed by the compelling truth of the directee's life, and truth emerges for both partners. Because they stand within a common faith tradition, the directee's story can become a contemporary form of "gospel" witness for the director. Finally, the spiritual direction situation can become a "sacramental" experience for the director as well as for the directee.

Conclusion

It remains only to retrace the twistings and turnings of this argument through the course of these reflections on narrative in spiritual direction with a view to bringing into sharper focus the path traversed.

Chapter One opened with a quotation from the *The Book of Privy Counselling* which expressed the longing, the need, and the help which one Christian can render another by receiving the story of a self interacting with the strangely loving and utterly mysterious reality of God. This help I identified as spiritual direction and traced the history of this ancient and perennial practice through six models. Of particular relevance to the emergence of the contemporary model of spiritual direction were the desert model and the late-medieval, non-monastic model which were precursors to the charismatic and non-institutional model operative today. Finally, Chapter One began to identify the narrative aspect within spiritual direction as the stories that directees offer in order to share their experiences with a director.

Chapter Two provided two examples of the progress of spiritual direction conversations. These cases were themselves narrative constructions illustrating how people relate experiences significant to spiritual growth through narrative. In both cases, the experience selected was that of spiritual direction. Secondly, through the verbatim exchanges reconstructed in the cases, the reader was able to imagine what transpires in spiritual direction and, in a sense, could plausibly fill in some of the narrative blanks as my analysis proceeded.

Chapter Three placed the narrative analysis of spiritual direction processes within the larger framework of philosophical hermeneutics. The director and directee are both engaged in a hermeneutical process through elaborating and interpreting the directee's narrative. Gadamer's analysis of a genuine conversation as a model for the hermeneutical process was particularly illuminating since the interpretive activity of spiritual direction ordinarily takes place within a conversation. Further Gadamer's hermeneutical theory provided a helpful way for understanding the role of tradition and the complex exercise and development of *phronesis.*

Chapter Four elaborated a theoretical framework for establishing reasons why narrative forms of discourse are required to account for fundamental aspects of human experience. This chapter defined narrative, identified its salient characteristics, and explored the relationship between narrative form and the narrative quality of human experience. Foremost among these characteristics is the correspondence of the human experience of history to the linguistic form of narrative which creates a coherent unity through time. Finally, the role of metaphorical forms of expression within spiritual direction narratives was described because metaphorical language is required in order to convey religious experiences at all.

Chapter Five further developed the theoretical framework of narrative appropriate to the spiritual direction conversation. Central to spiritual direction narratives is the narrative construction of personal and communal identity, especially spiritual identity. Secondly, additional effects of this type of storytelling were discovered to result from the narrative process itself. Because stories and storytelling create and maintain "world," the directee's narrative activity is one way a Christian creates an ongoing sense of world. Finally, Chapter Five suggested several practical strategies of director response to the directee's narratives consonant with narrative theory.

Chapter Six engaged in a literary critical, genre analysis of spiritual direction narratives. These were identified as an oral, confidential, serial mode of spiritual autobiography. The master story of spiritual direction is a story of faith which is both the horizon of all the storytelling and the subject of spiritual direction narratives. Particular attention was given to gender differences in narrative styles. Finally, the role of the director as "implied reader" within the directee's narrative construction was made explicit.

The first part of Chapter Seven focused briefly on the effect of the directee's storytelling on the director. Again, Gadamer's hermeneutical theory was used to illuminc the director's participation in the directee's project of self-understanding. The director finds himself or herself addressed by the directee's faith witness and the compelling truth of this story. The director participates in the directee's story by the activity of following it and constructing his or her meaning in response. Finally, participation in the directee's story may become an experience of communion, of shared life with the directee and a shared experience of God within the direction session itself.

Throughout, my primary intention has been to articulate and illuminate the actual narrative elements in the spiritual direction conversation. Some practical implications for spiritual direction follow from this narrative analysis. It seems to me that many contemporary directors draw exclusively from psychological theories and models and/or theological categories rather than from a narrative model. I propose that the practice of spiritual direction could be enhanced by a director's ability to understand the narrative processes elaborated in this study, to foster the directee's growth in the spiritual life by responding explicitly to these narratives and to enhance the actual effects of this activity in a positive way. Essentially, such responses are an intelligent act of the imagination placed at the service of the directee's growth.

Notes

Chapter One

[1] *The Book of Privy Counselling,* trans. William Johnston (Garden City, New York: Doubleday, 1973), pp. 182–83.

[2] Denis Edwards, *Human Experience of God* (New York: Paulist Press, 1983), p. 28 or Karl Rahner, *Foundations of Christian Faith* (New York: Seabury Press, 1978), pp. 81–89.

[3] See Sandra Schneiders, "Horizons on Spiritual Direction," *Horizons* 11 (Spring 1984):100–111 for a review of recent books on this subject.

[4] For the history of spiritual direction, see Edouard des Places, "Direction Spirituelle," *Dictionnaire de Spiritualité,* vol. 3, cols. 1002–1214; Kenneth Leech, *Soul Friend: The Practice of Christian Spirituality* (San Francisco: Harper and Row, 1980), pp. 34–89; John T. McNeill, *A History of the Cure of Souls* for a general treatment of the history of sacramental confession with relevance to spiritual guidance; and Jerome Neufelder and Mary Coelho, eds., *Writings on Spiritual Direction by Great Christian Masters* (New York: Seabury Press, 1982). For readers interested in a more detailed treatment of these models of spiritual direction, consult the microfilm version of this manuscript for extensive documentation from primary sources: *Narrative Aspects of Spiritual Direction,* (Ann Arbor, Michigan: University Microfilms, 1986).

[5] "The abba did not give 'spiritual direction'; if asked, he would give a 'word' which would become a sacrament to the hearer. The action of God was paramount and the only point of such 'words' was to free the disciple to be led by the Spirit of God, just as the abba himself would. In the desert there could only be one father to a disciple and even when he died, he was still the father of his sons. There was no need to change fathers, or to find a new one if one died. It was a lasting and permanent relationship. In such a relationship, tradition was passed on by life as well as by word; those who had already been a certain way into the experience of the monastic life must be able to become this channel of grace to others. But the aim was always for the abba to disappear. The real guide was the Holy Spirit, who would be given to those who learned to receive him." Benedicta Ward, "Spiritual Direction in the Desert Fathers," *The Way* 24 (January 1984):66. Here and wherever non-inclusive language is regrettably used in citations I have retained the original wording of the authors.

[6] "Spiritual Fatherhood in the Literature of the Desert," in John R. Sommerfeldt, ed., *Abba: Guides to Wholeness and Holiness, East and West* (Kalamazoo: Cistercian Publications, 1982), p. 42.

[7] Ibid., p. 45.

[8] Ward, p. 65.

[9] Here and elsewhere charismatic means that the person was accredited for the task of spiritual direction by the direct action of the Holy Spirit. Consequently, this task and responsibility of spiritual direction is a gift received from the Holy Spirit in contrast to the responsibility of an office such as presbyteral ordination or the office of abbot/abbess conferred by human institutions.

[10] *The Sayings of the Fathers,* trans. Owen Chadwick in *Western Asceticism* (Philadelphia: Westminster Press, 1958), records this anecdote: "An old man, who had a proved disci-

ple, once turned him out in a fit of irritation. The disciple sat down outside to wait; and the old man found him there when he opened the door, and did penance to him, saying: 'You are my Father because your humility and patience have conquered the weakness of my soul. Come inside: now you are the old father, and I am the young disciple; my age must give way to your conduct' " (#17, p. 179).

[11] Ward, p. 65.

[12] Benedict of Nursia wrote his Rule sometime after 525 while at Monte Cassino, Italy. This Rule formed the basis of Benedictine and Cistercian (a reform dating from the late eleventh and twelfth centuries) life.

[13] The relevant articles in the rule are: Chapter Two, "The Qualities of the Abbot," and Chapter Sixty-Four, "The Election of an Abbot." Timothy Fry, ed., *The Rule of St. Benedict in Latin and English with Notes* (Collegeville, Minnesota: The Liturgical Press, 1981).

[14] *The Golden Epistle,* trans. Theodore Berkeley (Kalamazoo: Cistercian Publications, 1980), #51. See ##53–54 and ##98–103 for further advice on the novice/spiritual father relationship.

[15] Ibid., #239.

[16] William of St. Thierry, *Exposition on the Song of Songs,* trans. Mother Columba Hart (Shannon: Irish University Press, 1969), #58.

[17] The Fourth Lateran Council (1215) prescribed a rule of annual confession of sin for "every faithful of either sex who has reached the age of discretion . . . in secret to his own priest" (Denzinger, #812).

[18] The scope of the abbesses' spiritual leadership was extensive. "Women did exercise direct 'clerical' authority in the thirteenth century (preaching, hearing confessions from nuns under them, and bestowing blessings). . . . But such things were increasingly criticized and suppressed." Caroline Walker

Bynum, *Jesus as Mother: Studies in the Spirituality of the High Middle Ages* (Berkeley: University of California Press, 1982), pp. 15–16 and her notes 14 and 15.

[19] *The Westminster Dictionary of Christian Spirituality,* ed. Gordon S. Wakefield (1983) s.v. "Dominican Spirituality, Dominicans," by Simon Tugwell.

[20] These were groups composed of women who chose ". . . to set themselves apart from the world by living austere, poor lives in which manual labor and service were joined to worship. . . . At least initially they contrasted sharply with traditional monasticism by taking no vows and having no complex organization and rules, no order linking the houses, no hierarchy of officials and no wealthy founders or leaders." Bynum, p. 14.

[21] "Direction Spirituelle," DS, vol. 3, col. 1083.

[22] Auguste Poulain defines supernatural ecstasy this way: ". . . a state that not only at the outset, but during its whole existence, contains two essential elements: the first, which is interior and invisible, is a very intense attention to some religious subject; the second, which is corporeal and visible, is the alienation of the sensible faculties." *The Graces of Interior Prayer: A Treatise on Mystical Theology,* trans. from the 6th ed. Leonora Smith (St. Louis: Herder, 1949), p. 243. Caroline Bynum asserts that publicly observable ecstasy gave these people "religious power" which contrasted with the power of office that clerics held. Through eucharistic ecstasy they achieved "union with God in the central moment of mediation and thereby became mediators (of God) themselves. Thus they became . . . preachers, touchers of God, vessels within which God appeared." *Jesus as Mother,* pp. 257–59.

[23] Hadewijch of Antwerp, *Hadewijch: the Complete Works,* trans. Mother Columba Hart (New York: Paulist Press, 1980), p. 78.

[24] Margery Kempe, *The Book of Margery Kempe,* ed.

Sandford Meech and Hope Allen (Oxford: Oxford University Press, 1961), p. 42.

[25] Kenelm Foster and Mary John Ronayne, eds. and trans., *I, Catherine: Selected Writings of St. Catherine of Siena* (London: Collins, 1980), p. 15.

[26] Hadewijch's writings consisted of Letters, Poems in Stanzas, Visions, and Poems in Couplets compiled in *The Complete Works.* Julian of Norwich wrote *Showings,* trans. Edmund Colledge and James Walsh (New York: Paulist Press, 1978). Catherine of Siena dictated *The Dialogue,* trans. Suzanne Noffke (New York: Paulist Press, 1980), to Raymond of Capua, her secretary. For her letters see *le Lettere di s. Caterina da Siena,* ed. P. Misciatelli, 4 vols. (Florence: G. Barbera, 1860). Catherine of Genoa's teaching was compiled by her disciple, Ettore Vernazza, after her death. Cf. Catherine of Genoa, *Purgation and Purgatory, the Spiritual Dialogue,* trans. Serge Hughes (New York: Paulist Press, 1979).

[27] Thomas of Cantimpré, the Dominican prior of Louvain, referred to St. Lutgard of Aywières (d. 1246) as his *mater specialissima* and James of Vitry "regularly calls Mary of Oignies (d. 1213) his *mater spiritualis.*" Paul Mommaers, "Hadewijch in Conflict," no date (xeroxed), p. 21.

[28] Gerard J. Campbell briefly describes the structure and process of these exercises: "The First Week is preceded by a kind of preamble called First Principle and Foundation. This is a consideration concerning creation, the purpose of life, and the proper relationship of a person to the rest of creation. The First Week is devoted to prayer about sin and its consequences. The Second Week begins with a contemplation of Christ's kingship over the world. There follows a series of contemplations on the mysteries of Christ's life up to the Last Supper. During this week various exercises are proposed to assist the retreatant to make choices about the direction of his or her life or about a better fulfillment of choices already

made. The Third Week brings the retreatant to share in the sufferings and death of Jesus and to appreciate his saving love in the passion. Finally the Fourth Week leads the retreatant to an experience of the joy Jesus shared with his followers in his Risen life. The concluding exercise is a profound and intimate experience of the many gifts of God's love to the individual and an invitation to an appropriate response of love in return." *The Westminster Dictionary,* s.v. "The Spiritual Exercises."

[29] Ignatius of Loyola, *The Spiritual Exercises,* trans. Louis J. Puhl (Chicago: Loyola University Press, 1951), #1.

[30] *The Spiritual Exercises of St. Ignatius of Loyola with a Commentary and "Directorium in Exercitia,"* trans. W. H. Longridge (London: Roxburgh House, 1919).

[31] Ignatius' term for the one who makes the Exercises.

[32] See also supplementary information on these points in *The Directory to the Spiritual Exercises,* Chapters 2, 5, 8 and 9.

[33] Ernest Larkin describes discernment of spirits this way: "It [discernment] seeks to read the movements of the sensible and spiritual affectivity in a positive way, i.e. as signs of the influence of the Spirit or a counter-force. This is possible in the Second Week, because the affectivity now registers in an immediate, uncensored way the reaction of the whole person. Specifically the feelings now show the consonance or dissonance between the present experience and the spiritual orientation of the person. The criteriology of these affective responses is precisely the tradition of the discernment." *The Westminster Dictionary,* s.v. "Discernment of Spirits."

[34] See *Exercises,* nos. 2 and 15.

[35] See also the *Directory,* chapter 7 and 2.7.

[36] See Joseph de Guibert, *The Jesuits: Their Spiritual Doctrine and Practice,* trans. William J. Young from the 1953 ed. (Chicago: Institute of Jesuit Sources, 1964), pp. 310–11.

[37] This ecumenical council was primarily concerned with elaborating the Catholic response to the challenge of the Protestant Reformation.

[38] "Ask your spiritual director to prescribe your acts of devotion, for this will double their value and merit; for over and above their intrinsic value, Philothea, they will have the merit of being done under obedience." Francis De Sales, *Introduction to the Devout Life*, trans. Michael Day (Westminster, Maryland: Newman Press, 1956), p. 122.

[39] Adolphe Tanquérey, *The Spiritual Life: A Treatise on Ascetical and Mystical Theology*, trans. Herman Branderis (Westminster, Maryland: Newman Press, 1930), p. 11. This manual of ascetical and mystical theology represented the culmination of this whole approach to the spiritual life from the sixteenth century to the first part of the twentieth century.

[40] Ibid., pp. 22–23.

[41] Thomas Merton, "The Spiritual Father in the Desert Tradition," in *Contemplation in a World of Action* (Garden City, New York: Doubleday, 1965), p. 282.

[42] Leech, *Soul Friend,* p. 58.

[43] Tanquérey, p. 257. "God, who established His Church as a hierarchical society, has willed that souls be sanctified through submission to the Sovereign Pontiff and to the Bishops in things external, and to confessors in things internal." The duties of penitents flow from this same view of authority. "Penitents will see in their spiritual director the person of Our Lord Himself. If it is true that all authority comes from God, it is more so of the authority the priest exercises over consciences in the confessional. The power of binding and loosing, of opening and closing the gates of heaven, of guiding souls in the paths of perfection, is a divine power and cannot reside outside him who is the lawful representative, the ambassador of Christ. . . . This is the principle from which all

duties toward a spiritual director flow—respect, trust, docility." Tanquérey, p. 267.

[44] "Listen to him, then, as though he were an angel from heaven sent to guide you there." De Sales, p. 16.

[45] "Some souls do see their way before them far better than others, and therefore do move fewer questions. The instructor therefore is to . . . instruct his disciples how they may themselves find out the way proper for them, by observing themselves what doeth good and what causeth harm to their spirits; in a word, that he is only God's usher . . ." Dom Augustine Baker, *Holy Wisdom,* ed. Serenus Cressy from *Sancta Sophia* (Wheathampstead: Anthony Clarke, 1972), p. 57. See John of the Cross, *Living Flame of Love,* chapter 3, ##30–62 in *The Collected Works of St. John of the Cross,* trans. Kieran Kavanaugh and Otilio Rodriguez (Washington: ICS Publications, 1973) for a description of the role of the director and the harm done by incompetence. See chapters 13, 4, 29, and elsewhere in *The Life of Teresa of Jesus,* trans. E. Allison Peers (Garden City, New York: Doubleday, 1960), for her assessment of spiritual directors.

[46] Tanquérey, pp. 22 and 270.

[47] Thérèse of Lisieux, *Story of a Soul,* trans. John Clarke (Washington: ICS Publications, 1976), pp. 150–51.

[48] "A man of wide experience, Father Desurmont, writes as follows on this subject (directing women). . . . 'Let there be nothing savoring of feeling, either in manner or gesture, nor the least shadow of familiarity. As to conversations, no more than is necessary; as to dealings outside of matters of conscience, only those that have a recognized serious purpose. As much as possible, let there be no direction outside the confessional, and no correspondence. They must not be made even to suspect that one is personally interested in them. Their mentality is so constituted that if they be led to think them-

selves the object of a particular regard or affection, almost without fail, they descend to a natural plane, be it through vanity or sentimentality.' " Tanquérey, #546 c, p. 265.

[49] The titles of three volumes on the subject of spiritual direction reflect this concern for acceptable images, especially in non-Roman Catholic circles. See Leech, *Soul Friend;* Tilden Edwards, *Spiritual Friend: Reclaiming the Gift of Spiritual Direction* (New York: Paulist Press, 1980); and Morton T. Kelsey, *Companions on the Inner Way: The Art of Spiritual Guidance* (New York: Paulist Press, 1983).

[50] Sandra Schneiders and Nemeck and Coombs exemplify attempts to redefine the terminology in an acceptable way. "Spiritual direction can be understood as a process, carried out in a one-to-one interpersonal context, of establishing and maintaining a growth-orientation (that is, direction) in one's faith life. This process has two moments which are in constant dialectical relationship with each other, namely, listening to and articulating God's call in one's life, and progressively elaborating an integrated and adequate response to that call." Schneiders, "The Contemporary Ministry of Spiritual Direction," *Chicago Studies* 15 (Spring 1976):123. Likewise, Francis Kelly Nemeck and Marie Theresa Coombs assert, "The spiritual director . . . helps bring into consciousness and explicate the already existing spiritual direction in which the Spirit is leading the directee." *The Way of Spiritual Direction* (Wilmington, Delaware: Michael Glazier, 1985), p. 31.

[51] Two other definitions of spiritual direction in the contemporary context emphasize different aspects. Barry and Connolly offer an experiential definition: "We define Christian spiritual direction, then, as help given by one Christian to another which enables that person to pay attention to God's personal communication to him or her, to respond to this personally communicating God, to grow in intimacy with this God, and to live out the consequences of the relationship."

William A. Barry and William J. Connolly, *The Practice of Spiritual Direction* (New York: Seabury Press, 1982), p. 8. Schneiders further defines direction as ". . . a process carried out in the context of a one-to-one relationship in which a competent guide helps a fellow Christian to grow in the spiritual life by means of personal encounters that have the directee's spiritual growth as their explicit object." "Contemporary Ministry," p. 124.

[52] The relationship of spiritual direction to narrative has been previously addressed by Robert F. Morneau. "The Spiritual Director as Literary Critic," *Review for Religious* (March/April 1985):220–32. Morneau's treatment of the spiritual director as literary critic works from analogy describing similarities between the two terms. However, he never argues for the fundamental narrativity of the spiritual direction situation itself.

Chapter Three

[1] Throughout this discussion, the situation envisioned is that of the two-party conversation. In the retreat situation sessions are usually daily while ongoing spiritual direction sessions are usually every three to four weeks.

[2] Hans-Georg Gadamer, *Truth and Method* (New York: Crossroad, 1975), p. 340.

[3] Ibid., p. 248.

[4] Ibid., pp. 330–31.

[5] Ibid., pp. 249–51.

[6] It is this realization of the extremely important role of the story form of communication from the beginnings of Christianity that has given rise to various attempts and approaches to what is called narrative theology.

[7] Robert Alter, *The Art of Biblical Narrative* (New York: Basic Books, Inc., 1981), p. 14.

[8] Eric Auerbach makes the claim that biblical narrative influenced the secular literary tradition in the direction of realism. On the other hand, a non-Christian literary form, the journey, was adopted and adapted by Augustine creating the confessional form. Later literary forms of autobiography eventually omit a spiritual purpose. *Mimesis: The Representation of Reality in Western Literature,* trans. Willard R. Trask (Princeton: Princeton University Press, 1953).

[9] Auerbach, ibid., p. 62.

[10] Gadamer, ibid., pp. 236–40.

[11] Ibid., p. 269.

[12] Barrett J. Mandel, "Full of Life Now," in *Autobiography: Essays Theoretical and Critical,* ed. James Olney (Princeton: Princeton University Press, 1980), pp. 68–69.

[13] Ibid., pp. 269–72.

[14] Ibid., p. 261.

[15] See for example the work of Elisabeth Schüssler Fiorenza, *In Memory of Her* (New York: Crossroad, 1983), or Rosemary Radford Ruether, *Sexism and God-Talk* (Boston: Beacon Press, 1983), and *New Woman/New Earth* (New York: Seabury Press, 1975) among others.

[16] Gadamer, p. 278.

[17] For Gadamer's treatment of Aristotle see ibid., pp. 278–89.

[18] Discernment is the name usually given to this kind of exercise of practical decision-making in the Christian religious tradition.

[19] Gadamer, p. 288.

[20] Counseling theory names this ability to think with and companion another in a concrete situation "empathy." See Gerard Egan, *The Skilled Helper* (Monterey, California: Brooks/Cole Publishing Company, 1975), pp. 76–90.

Chapter Four

[1] For an excellent critical evaluation of various approaches to narrative theology see Michael Goldberg, *Narrative and Theology: A Critical Introduction* (Nashville: Abingdon, 1982).

[2] Barbara Herrnstein Smith asserts that every narrative is constructed in relationship to the interrelated factors of (1) a concrete teller, (2) an occasion of the telling, and (3) the human purposes, perceptions, actions, or interactions that occur in a face-to-face mode of narration. "Narrative Versions, Narrative Theories," in *On Narrative,* ed. W. T. J. Mitchell (Chicago: University of Chicago Press, 1981), pp. 217 and 222.

[3] For the most part, the terms "narrative" and "story" will be used in an interchangeable way although some literary critics make a distinction between narrative and story. See Robert Scholes, "Language, Narrative, Anti-Narrative," in *On Narrative, Narrative* (New York: Oxford University Press, 1966), p. 4, for their discussion of this distinction and precise definitions from a literary critical perspective.

[4] Paul Ricoeur described two of the most salient features of all narrative as "sequence and pattern," or a combination of a chronological dimension with a non-chronological one. It is this second dimension of narrative which construes "significant wholes out of scattered events." It is this patterning, accomplished in the telling of a story or a series of related events, that gives this narrational activity the character of a reflective judgment. "To tell and to follow a story is already to *reflect upon* events in order to encompass them in successive wholes." Paul Ricoeur, "The Narrative Function," *Semeia* 13 (1978):183–85. For Ricoeur's extended analysis of emplotment, see *Time and Myth,* 2 vols., trans. Kathleen McLauglin

and David Pellauer (Chicago: University of Chicago Press, 1983), 1:Chapter Two, pp. 31–51.

⁵ See Scholes and Kellogg, *The Nature of Narrative,* (New York: Harper, 1966), chapter 7, and Wayne C. Booth, *The Rhetoric of Fiction,* 2nd ed. (Chicago: University of Chicago Press, 1983), chapters 7–10. See also Susan Snaider Lanser, *The Narrative Act: Point of View in Prose Fiction* (Princeton, New Jersey: Princeton University Press, 1981), pp. 13–14.

⁶ Northrop Frye names this phenomenon "explanation by emplotment." *Anatomy of Criticism* (New Jersey: Princeton University Press, 1957), pp. 353–54.

⁷ Ricoeur explains the relationship between explanation and plot in the writing of history. "The historian . . . does not merely tell a story. He makes an entire set of events, considered as a whole, *into* a story." "The Narrative Function," p. 189. He returns to this theme and develops it in more detail in *Time and Narrative,* vol. 1., pp. 161–74.

⁸ James Hillman, "The Fiction of Case History," in *Healing Fiction* (Barrytown, New York: Station Hill, 1983), pp. 9–10.

⁹ Ricoeur, "Narrative Function," p. 182.

¹⁰ Michael Novak, *Ascent of the Mountain, Flight of the Dove* (San Francisco: Harper and Row, 1971), p. 49.

¹¹ Stephen Crites, "The Narrative Quality of Experience," *The Journal of the American Academy of Religion* 39 (September 1971):291–311.

¹² Ibid., p. 291.

¹³ Ibid., p. 292.

¹⁴ Ibid., p. 294.

¹⁵ See Crites' distinction between what he calls "sacred" stories and "mundane" ones. Ibid., pp. 295–97.

¹⁶ Ibid.

¹⁷ Ray Hart discusses this same phenomenon as "the coinherence of the modes of time" giving particular emphasis

to the role of active imagination in memory of the past and in anticipation of the future. Ray Hart, *Unfinished Man and the Imagination* (New York: Seabury Press, 1979), pp. 188ff.

[18] Crites, p. 298.

[19] Ibid., pp. 300–301.

[20] Gadamer contrasts memory with "retention." Retention corresponds to Crites' simple recall. And for Gadamer, memory is more than simply a capacity, but belongs to the finite historical being of man. "Remembering, forgetting, and recalling belong to the historical constitution of man and are themselves part of his history. . . . Memory must be formed; for memory is not memory for anything and everything. One has a memory for many things, and not for others; one wants to preserve one thing in memory and banish another. . . . Forgetting belongs within the context of remembering and recalling in a way that has long been ignored; forgetting is not merely an absence and a lack but . . . a condition of the life of mind. Only by forgetting does the mind have the chance of total renewal, the capacity to see everything with fresh eyes, so that what is long familiar combines with the new into a many levelled unity." Gadamer, *Truth and Method,* p. 16.

[21] Gadamer also reflects on the dialectical nature of experience. "We use the word 'experience' in two different senses: to refer to the experiences that fit in with our expectations and confirm it, and to the experience we have. This latter, 'experience' in the real sense, is always negative. If we have an experience of an object, this means that we have not seen the thing correctly hitherto and now know it better." Ibid., p. 317.

[22] Others develop the importance of embodiment more completely than Crites. For instance, Jerry H. Gill, drawing on Merleau-Ponty's work on perception, gives this description: "A . . . way of bringing out the essential quality of our embodied existence is in terms of the notion of *fulcrum*. Not only does our world come to us as revolving around us, but we

encounter and/or engage it in and through our bodies as the pivot or leverage point of the activity dimension of our existence. Our bodies serve as the juncture at which we interact with and affect the world. We move toward and into our world through our bodies, just as it moves toward and engages us through our bodies. For the obvious but nonetheless amazing fact is that our bodies are *both* us *and* part of the world. Our existence is constituted by them and their existence is constituted by the world." Jerry H. Gill, *On Knowing God* (Philadelphia: Westminster Press, 1981), pp. 70–71.

[23] This less organized form of consciousness has frequently been imitated in the modern technique of "stream of consciousness" which reconstructs a more fragmented focus of attention in which sensations, thoughts, and feelings interpose themselves between the events of the plot. Although this form of consciousness does not organize itself into a single unified story with all of the details relating to the main narrative line, it is still organized at least by the temporal succession of before and after.

[24] Novak, p. 49.

[25] Denis Edwards, *The Human Experience of God* (New York: Paulist Press, 1983), p. 7.

[26] Ibid.

[27] Edward Schillebeeckx, *Christ the Experience of Jesus as Lord,* trans. John Bowden (New York: Crossroad, 1981), p. 33.

[28] In this section "pre-conceptual" corresponds to the tacit or skill dimension as Michael Polanyi defines it. As an epistemological concept, it is not entirely synonymous with Gadamer's term "prejudice."

[29] "Although the expert diagnostician, taxonomist and cotton-classer can indicate their clues and formulate their maxims, they know many more things than they can tell, knowing them only in practice, as instrumental particulars,

and not explicitly as objects." Michael Polanyi, *Personal Knowledge: Towards a Post-Critical Philosophy* (Chicago: University of Chicago Press, 1958), p. 88.

[30] Schillebeeckx describes the interrelationship between "objective" and "subjective" elements in experience in this way: "Our real experiences are neither purely objective nor purely subjective. At least partially, there is something which is 'given,' which we cannot completely manipulate or change; in experience we have an offer of reality. On the other hand, it is not purely objective; for the experience is filled out and colored by the reminiscences and sensibilities, concepts and longings of the person who has the experience. Thus the irreducible elements of our experiences form a totality which already contains interpretation. We experience in the act of interpreting, without being able to draw a neat distinction between the element of experience and the element of interpretation." Schillebeeckx, *Christ,* p. 33.

[31] This last function of narrative reveals the rhetorical character of narration. George A. Kennedy gives this description of rhetoric: "Rhetoric is a form of communication. The author of a communication has some kind of purpose, and rhetoric certainly includes the ways by which he seeks to accomplish that purpose. . . . Purposes cover a whole spectrum from converting hearers to a view opposed to that they previously held, to implanting a conviction not otherwise considered, to deepening belief in a view already favorably entertained, to a demonstration of the cleverness of the author, to teaching or exposition. In practice almost every communication is rhetorical in that it uses some device to try to affect the thought, actions, or emotions of an audience, but the degree of rhetoric varies enormously." *Classical Rhetoric and its Christian and Secular Tradition from Ancient to Modern Times* (Chapel Hill: University of North Carolina Press, 1980), p. 4. Directees employ rhetoric consciously or uncon-

sciously in the spiritual direction dialogue which is not unlike other forms of communication. Directees certainly want the director to find their stories plausible and convincing and will shape their narratives to include the director's interests. It is even not unusual for a directee to make a narrative lively and entertaining especially if the event in question is problematic or painful. However, if a directee is unable to minimize attempts at persuading the director that his or her narrative interpretation of an experience is the only possible way that event can be understood, the process of spiritual direction may be seriously impaired.

[32] See Chapter 5, "Helping a Person Notice and Share with the Lord Key Interior Facts," in William A. Barry, S. J., and William J. Connolly, S. J., *The Practice of Spiritual Direction* (New York: Seabury Press, 1982) for further discussion of this process in spiritual direction. Although the authors' discussion emphasizes an early stage of spiritual direction, it is my experience that many mature and experienced people are helped by attention to this kind of noticing.

[33] In the lyric form, the writer is able to condense into the images and symbols of the poem a highly complex, multivalent reality. Frequently, the lyric deals with a small slice of experience, a momentary awareness or complex perception. Because the lyric poem relies on metaphorical expression as its primary vehicle for conveying meaning, it is strongly tied to the world of actual sense impressions. The poet helps the reader/listener see or experience his or her perception and response to something through the descriptive power of sensory language. Lyric poetry functions directly as an "interpretation of the raw, loose universe." See Annie Dillard, *Living by Fiction* (New York: Harper and Row, 1982), p. 147.

[34] Ignatius of Loyola, *Spiritual Exercises,* trans. Louis Puhl (Chicago: Loyola University Press, 1951), ##190–199.

[35] Mary's case, p. 36.

[36] This is one form Ignatius' technique of "repetition" may take. "We should pay attention to and dwell upon those points in which we experienced greater consolation or desolation or greater spiritual appreciation." *Exercises,* #62.

[37] Working with images in this way may not necessarily be an experience of God for everyone. It is, however, a helpful form of meditation for many people and a powerful tool for psychological and spiritual growth which in recent times C. J. Jung taught as the process of "active imagination."

[38] This is the classical definition of "contemplation" in the western mystical tradition which teaches a union in love with God that is characterized by the inability to grasp God by knowledge or imagination or by any activity whatever but that is available to a person through an obscure, general awareness in knowledge or love or both of God. See John of the Cross, *The Ascent of Mount Carmel,* Book II, 13 and 14 in *The Collected Works,* or Thomas Merton, *Contemplative Prayer* (New York: Doubleday, 1971), Chapter 14 for a series of quotations from the tradition describing and explaining this experience.

[39] St. John of the Cross, *Ascent* and *The Dark Night* in *The Collected Works,* and Pseudo-Dionysius, *The Divine Names and the Mystical Theology,* trans. C. E. Rolt, Translations of Christian Literature, Series 1: Greek Texts (New York: Macmillan, 1920); Gregory of Nyssa. *The Life of Moses,* trans. Everett Ferguson and Abraham J. Malherbe (New York: Paulist Press, 1978).

[40] Teresa of Avila several times distinguishes among different kinds of prayer by comparison with sleep. See Chapters 3.11, 4.86 in *The Interior Castle,* trans. Kieran Kavanaugh, O.C.D. and Otilio Rodriguez, O.C.D. (New York: Paulist Press, 1979) and elsewhere.

[41] See John of the Cross, *The Spiritual Canticle* in *The Collected Works,* Teresa of Avila, *The Interior Castle,* and

Pierre Adnés, "Mariage Spirituel," *Dictionnaire de Spiritualité*, vol. 10, cols. 388–408 (Paris: Beauchesne, 1980).

[42] Maureen Conroy records this case in "A Dwelling
Place: Images and Our Experience of God," *Studies in Formative Spirituality* 6 (February 1985):20–21.

[43] Avery Dulles, *Models of the Church* (New York: Doubleday, 1978), pp. 24–25.

[44] Philip Wheelwright, *Metaphor and Reality* (Bloomington: Indiana University Press, 1962), pp. 92–110.

[45] See Kathleen Fischer, *The Inner Rainbow: The Imagination and the Christian Life* (New York: Paulist Press, 1983),
pp. 92–95.

[46] Archetypal symbols are those which seem to be univer-
sally shared by all people regardless of culture or historical
period. These symbols tend to be rooted in every day human
experience in the physical and social world. C. G. Jung drew
on these collective patterns in history and culture to formulate
his psychological theory of the archetypes and the unconscious. Among the archetypes Jung emphasized as ways of
symbolizing psychic processes were the following: light and
darkness, the Persona, the Shadow, the Self, the Anima and
Animus, the Trickster, the Divine Child, animals, the Great
Mother and the Great Father, the Wise Old People, Sacrifice,
the Mandala, the Spiral, the Perilous Journey, and Death and
Rebirth. See C. G. Jung, *The Archetypes and the Collective
Unconscious*, vol. 9.1 in *The Collected Works of C. G. Jung*,
Bollingen Series XX (London: Routledge and Kegan Paul,
1959).

[47] Bernard Cooke talks about this development of personal symbols. "For each of us there are certain things, places,
persons, or events that have become specially meaningful and
that continue to say something special to us whenever we
remember them or encounter them again.

"In this process of symbols emerging in our consciousness as retainers and transmitters of meaning, a central role is played by our memory. It is because we can recall past happenings, relive them (sometimes with great vividness) in our imagination, re-experience the joy or anguish or achievements of the past, that these can still affect our awareness and our emotions. Along with this, we have the ability, through creative imagination, of sharing vicariously in the meaningful experiences of others. We do this when we see a movie or read a novel or listen to a friend relate a harrowing experience he or she has just passed through.

"Because symbols have this power to touch the entire range of our consciousness—rational thought, imagination, emotions, dreams—they are a privileged means of expressing our most personal and important and disturbing experiences. The warm handshake of a dear friend, the singing of Christmas carols, . . . young lovers walking hand in hand— one could go on with a long list of symbols that speak to us on several levels of insight and feeling. Such symbols speak commonly to all of us and yet speak somewhat distinctively to all of us. When we reflect on it, we realize that such symbols do more than express how we think and feel; they are a powerful force in shaping the way we think and feel." Bernard Cooke, *Sacraments and Sacramentality* (Mystic, Conn.: Twenty-Third Publications, 1983), pp. 44–45.

[48] See James Olney, *Metaphors of the Self: Meaning in Autobiography* (Princeton: Princeton University Press, 1972.)

Chapter Five

[1] See George W. Stroup, "The Narrative Form of Personal Identity," in *The Promise of Narrative Theology,* (Atlanta: John Knox Press, 1981), pp. 102–105.

[2] Oliver Sacks, a neurosurgeon, poignantly describes the situation of patients who have suffered damage to the part of

the brain that supports this narrative construction of identity. Mr. Thompson continually created ". . . a world and self, to replace what was continually being forgotten and lost. Such a frenzy may call forth brilliant powers of invention and fancy . . . for such a patient *must literally make himself (and his world) up every moment.* We have each of us, a life story, an inner narrative—whose continuity, whose sense, *is* our lives. It might be said that each of us constructs and lives, a 'narrative', and that this narrative *is* us, our identities." *The Man Who Mistook His Wife for a Hat and Other Clinical Tales* (New York: Summit, 1985), p. 105.

³ Stroup, p. 111.

⁴ Steven Marcus gives an interesting account of the correlation of narrative accuracy with mental health in Freud's famous Case of Dora. ". . . Freud is implying that a coherent story is in some manner connected with mental health. . . . On this reading, human life is, ideally, a connected and coherent story, with all the details in explanatory place, and with everything (or as close to everything as is practically possible) accounted for, in its proper causal or other sequence. And inversely, illness amounts at least in part to suffering from an incoherent story or an inadequate narrative account of oneself." Steven Marcus, "Freud and Dora: Story, History, Case History," in *Representations: Essays on Literature and Society* (New York: Random House, 1975), pp. 276–77.

⁵ Jung seeks another story: "In many cases in psychiatry, the patient who comes to us has a story that is not told, and which as a rule no one knows of. To my mind, therapy only really begins after the investigation of that wholly personal story. It is the patient's secret, the rock against which he is shattered. If I know his secret story, I have a key to the treatment." C. G. Jung, *Memories, Dreams, and Reflections,* recorded and ed. Aniela Jaffé, trans. Richard and Clara Winston, 4th ed. (New York: Vintage, 1965), p. 117.

[6] John Navone and Thomas Cooper, *Tellers of the Word,* (New York: Le Jacq, 1981), p. 105.

[7] Feminist criticism of psychoanalytic theory and the theory of autobiography indicate that women's ego-consciousness differs from that of men. Women tend to develop ego-boundaries which are more permeable than men's. Their identities develop in such a way that they include service to others without threat to their own identities. In addition, because of a greater variety of social roles which women enact simultaneously, their autobiographies generally reflect what men would consider to be a fragmented consciousness rather than a highly unified one. Women tend to prefer the diary form which better represents their experience than the autobiography organized around a single dominant theme or role. See Jean Baker Miller, "Serving Others' Needs—Doing for Others," in *Toward a New Psychology of Women* (Boston: Beacon Press, 1978) and Carol Gilligan, *In a Different Voice* (Cambridge: Harvard University Press, 1982) for the psychological theory. For a feminist theory of autobiography, see Estelle C. Jelinek, "Introduction: Women's Autobiography and the Male Tradition," in *Women's Autobiography: Essays in Criticism,* ed. Jelinek (Bloomington: Indiana University Press, 1980), pp. 1–20, and Mary G. Mason, "The Other Voice: Autobiographies of Women Writers," in *Autobiography: Essays Theoretical and Critical,* ed. James Olney, pp. 207–35.

[8] Autobiographies are usually written only by those whose lives illuminate the issues, politics, philosophies, etc., of a given period of history in such a way that makes their lives significant for others. Critical studies of autobiography have discovered that to tell one's own story is an act of self-assertion which claims the right to define oneself on one's own terms. Socially disenfranchised groups tend to be rendered invisible as well as defined by the ways the enfranchised de-

scribe them in their stories. Through the opportunity to tell their story to someone who "counts" in their eyes ordinary or disenfranchised people discover that they actually have a valuable story to tell. Elizabeth Winston, "The Autobiographer and Her Readers: From Apology to Affirmation," *Women's Autobiography,* pp. 93–111. Anthropologist Barbara Myerhoff documents the effect of storytelling for members of a senior citizens center. Myerhoff, "Telling One's Story," *The Center Magazine* (March 1980):22–23.

[9] John M. Staudenmaier explicitly embraces the narrative dimension of spiritual direction as one way of counteracting this influence from technological culture. "United States Technology and Adult Commitment," *Studies in the Spirituality of Jesuits* 19 (January 1987):32–33.

[10] See Roy W. Fairchild, *Lifestory Conversations* (New York: United Presbyterian Church in the U.S.A., 1977). "Memory serves our sense of identity and continuity. To understand where we have been contributes to an understanding of where we are now and where we are going. . . . Each person is living out a unique, never to be repeated story. Unless one can survey accomplishments, regrets, high and low-points of past experience, the celebrations and the wildernesses, one cannot begin to perceive how God has been working in his/her story. . . . It is possible that a life which has been viewed as simply a series of individual happenings —as fragments, splinters, and broken off pieces—can be joined together in conversation by a thread of meaning that runs through them all" (pp. 14–15).

[11] As a hermeneutical activity, this process of constructing an identity by interpreting the whole in relationship to identifiable parts is one instance of what Gadamer calls "the hermeneutical circle" in which "the movement of understanding is constantly from the whole to the part and back to the whole." Gadamer, *Truth and Method,* p. 259.

[12] Barbara Herrnstein Smith suggests that fragmented recollection is only collected into a coherent whole in the concrete act of narrative. "Our knowledge of *past* events is usually *not* narrative in structure or given in story-like sequences: on the contrary, that knowledge is most likely to be in the form of general and imprecise recollections, scattered and possibly inconsistent pieces of verbal information, and various visual, auditory, and kinesthetic images—some of which, at any given time, will be more or less in or out of focus and all of which will be organized, integrated, and apprehended as a specific 'set' of events only in and through the very act by which we narrate them as such." Smith, "Narrative Versions, Narrative Theories," p. 225.

[13] Robert McAfee Brown suggests that most people live plural stories, some of which may conflict with the story God is trying to author with us in our lives: ". . . I not only *am* many stories, but I *have* many stories. . . . I am constantly balancing—or juggling—a number of ways of telling my own story: the masculine version, the American version, the human version, the Christian version, the university professor version, and so on. But I am also constantly reviewing those stories of my time: the feminine version, the Black version, the Third World version, the Jewish version, the blue collar version. . . . Within this multitude of stories, I accord one story, or several stories, a higher authority than others. . . . If things go well, my normative story is authenticated. . . . But things may not go well. My normative story may be . . . so badly challenged or shattered that I must painfully reconstruct a new story for myself." "My Story and 'the Story'," *Theology Today* 32 (July 1975):167.

[14] Carolyn Gratton, *Guidelines for Spiritual Direction,* p. 106.

[15] Brennan Manning, *A Stranger to Self-Hatred* (Denville, N.J.: Dimension Books, 1982), p. 95.

[16] See John Shea, *An Experience Named Spirit* (Chicago: Thomas More Press, 1983), pp. 102–104ff for an extended discussion of this process.

[17] See Stroup, pp. 116–17.

[18] Shea, p. 109.

[19] See Ignatius of Loyola, *The Exercises,* ##313 36; Ernest Larkin, *Silent Presence: Discernment as Process and Problem* (Denville, New Jersey: Dimension, 1981); and Jules Toner, *A Commentary of Saint Ignatius' Rules for the Discernment of Spirits* (St. Louis: Institute of Jesuit Sources, 1982) for more detailed discussion of discernment.

[20] See Neufelder and Coelho, pp. 117–24, for several classical and contemporary writers on this theme.

[21] N. Scott Momaday describes this quality of bonding and intimacy which occurred between him and his Kiowa grandmother: "When she told me those old stories, something strange and good and powerful was going on. I was a child, and that old woman was asking me to come directly into the presence of her mind and spirit; she was taking hold of my imagination, giving me to share in the great fortune of her wonder and delight. She was asking me to go with her to the confrontation of something that was sacred and eternal. It was a timeless, *timeless* thing; nothing of her old age or my childhood came between us." *House Made of Dawn* (New York: New American Library, 1968), p. 88. The kind of intimacy described above is certainly analogous to that which occurs between the director and the directee.

[22] Ray Hart, *Unfinished Man,* pp. 253–54.

[23] Frederick S. Perls, *Gestalt Therapy Verbatim* (Lafayette, Calif.: Real People Press, 1969).

[24] "It is a question of the form of attention we choose to bestow; of our willingness to see that in reading according to restricted codes we disregard as noise what, if read differently, patiently, would make another and rarer kind of sense."

Frank Kermode, "Secrets and Narrative Sequence," in *On Narrative,* p. 96. For an example of feminist criticism which reads the "secrets" in fiction by women writers, see Susan M. Gilbert and Susan Gubar, *Madwomen in the Attic* (New Haven: Yale University Press, 1979).

[25] Since suggesting an ending to someone else's story may also inhibit a timid directee, care must be exercised by the director. I find this procedure helpful when I begin to hear a repetitive pattern that indicates the directee is unknowingly stuck in a story that has negative consequences. I also find that projecting a variety of possible outcomes rather than only one alternative encourages the directee to entertain the possibility of an alternative outcome without the pressure to adopt one of my suggested endings.

[26] According to Paul Ricoeur, "To follow a story, then, is to understand the successive actions, thoughts, and feelings as having a *particular directedness.* By this I mean that we are pulled forward by the development and respond to this thrust with expectations concerning the outcome and the ending of the whole process. In this sense, the 'conclusion' of the story is the attracting pole of the process. But a narrative conclusion can be neither deduced nor predicted. No story without surprises, coincidences, encounters, revelations, recognitions, etc., would hold our attention. This is why we have to follow it *to the conclusion.* Instead of being predictable, a conclusion must be acceptable. Looking backward from the conclusion over the episodes which led up to it, we must be able to say that this end required those events and this chain of actions. Yet this backward glance is made possible by the teleologically guided movement of our expectations when we followed the story." "The Narrative Function," p. 182.

[27] Interview with Mary X, Bronx, New York, 7 May 1987.

[28] Work with symbols which arise from the directee's

narrative may be enhanced in a number of ways. Psycho-synthesis, as developed by Roberto Assagioli, *Psychosynthesis* (New York: Penguin, 1971), encourages people to visualize symbols which will foster their integration and development. One of the classic visualizations for cultivating spiritual development is the life cycle of the rose from seed to fully opened flower. Assagioli, pp. 214ff. See also Piero Ferucci, *What We May Be* (Los Angeles, Tarcher, 1982), pp. 117ff, for further development of this topic. If a director responds to images that emerge in the directee by suggesting visualization or painting, discernment is required in order to decide whether the effect of an image needs to be intensified or opposed. Images bear within them the possibility of encouraging development or regression.

[29] Wesley Kort, *Narrative Elements and Religious Meaning* (Philadelphia: Fortress Press, 1975), p. 35.

[30] Interview, 7 May 1987.

[31] Ibid.

[32] Gadamer, p. 252.

Chapter Six

[1] See Gerard Egan, *The Skilled Helper,* pp. 106–108 for an explanation of social influence theory.

[2] Carolyn Gratton, *Guidelines,* pp. 171–2.

[3] I am indebted to Professor Francis Houdek for this insight about the discovery of God in the search for self as it takes place in the context of spiritual direction. He said: "I think people come to direction with two reasons that get verbalized. And if direction goes with any fruitfulness, they find out the two reasons are the same. They come either to find themselves or to find God. And they work at direction from either one of those two perspectives. When they find themselves, they find God is very present. When they really dis-

cover God, in that whole process they find themselves." Interview with Francis Houdek, Berkeley, California, 18 January 1985.

[4] Roy Schafer, a neo-Freudian psychoanalyst, offers a particularly illuminating description of the storytelling process in psychoanalysis which captures both similarities to the narrative situation of spiritual direction and significant differences: ". . . we narrate others just as we narrate selves. The other person, like the self, is not something one has or encounters as such but an existence one tells. Consequently, telling 'others' about 'ourselves' is doubly narrative.

"Often the stories we tell about ourselves are life historical or autobiographical; we locate them in the past. For example, one might say, 'Until I was fifteen, I was proud of my father' or 'I had a totally miserable childhood.' These histories are present tellings. The same may be said of the histories we attribute to others. We change many implied or stated questions to which they are the answer. As a project in personal development, personal analysis changes the leading questions that one addresses to the tale of one's life and the lives of important others.

"People going through psychoanalysis, analysands, tell the analyst about themselves and others in the past and present. In making interpretations, the analyst retells these stories. In the retelling, certain features are accentuated while others are placed in parentheses; certain features are related to others in new ways or for the first time; some features are developed further, perhaps at great length. This retelling is done along psychoanalytic lines." Roy Schafer, *The Analytic Attitude* (New York: Basic Books, 1983), p. 219.

[5] One directee expressed a feeling of relief and joy at being able to explore explicitly the spiritual dimension of his experience. He had been in therapy for two years and reported that he could not explore the spiritual or moral dimension of

his mid-life crisis within the counseling situation because the therapist would not respond to this aspect of his experience. Although he could introduce the material, the therapist's non-engagement with it frustrated his attempts to incorporate his story of faith into his therapeutic story in that narrative situation.

[6] Scholes and Kellogg, *The Nature of Narrative,* p. 157.

[7] Barrett J. Mandel, "Full of Life Now," in *Autobiography: Essays Theoretical and Critical,* ed. Olney, p. 64.

[8] Formal autobiographies are "generally silent on intense feelings of hate, love, and fear, the disclosure of explicit sexual encounters, or the detailing of painful psychological experience." Estelle C. Jelinek, "Introduction: Women's Autobiography and the Male Tradition," p. 17.

[9] See Friedrich Wulf, "Spiritual Direction," *Sacramentum Mundi,* vol. 6, p. 166, and Francis Nemeck and Marie Therese Coombs, *The Way of Spiritual Direction,* p. 81.

[10] Wolfgang Iser describes the concept of the implied reader: "The concept of the implied reader is . . . a textual structure anticipating the presence of a recipient without necessarily defining him: This concept prestructures the role to be assumed by each recipient, and this holds true even when texts deliberately appear to ignore their possible recipient or actively excludes him. Thus the concept of the implied reader designates a network of response-inviting structures, which impel the reader to grasp the text.

"No matter who or what he may be the real reader is always offered a particular role to play, and it is this role that constitutes the concept of the implied reader." Wolfgang Iser, *The Act of Reading: A Theory of Aesthetic Response* (Baltimore: Johns Hopkins University Press, 1978), pp. 34–35. See also Wayne C. Booth, *The Rhetoric of Fiction,* chapters 5 and 6.

[11] See Iser, p. 96, for a discussion of the way textual

segments are presented to the reader's viewpoint in such a way that the reader becomes actively involved in constructing the connections between seemingly unrelated segments of the narrative.

[12] "The artful diarist who senses a kind of plot in his or her life will be selecting appropriate materials 'half-consciously'." Scholes and Kellogg, p. 211.

[13] Iser identifies four textual perspectives: narrator, character, plot, and reader. At any one moment, one of these perspectives becomes center stage. Iser calls the momentary focus on such a perspective a "theme." However, a "theme" is always set against a "horizon" which in this case encompasses all the other perspectives with which one was previously engaged. Iser, pp. 96–97.

[14] Scholes and Kellogg categorize "slice of life" and *cinéma verité* as empirical and mimetic forms of narration. They belong to representational narrative tending to emphasize mimesis more than plot. Scholes and Kellogg, p. 13.

[15] Ibid., p. 27.

[16] Scholes and Kellogg trace this cultural interest in the inward development of character as a primarily Christian element in our narrative literature. Ibid., p. 165. It seems that the director and perhaps the directee as well can construct this type of meaning for these narratives because one has already learned to follow this type of plot in one's experience of the novel.

[17] Iser asserts that "blanks" which cause a suspension of connectability in a story stimulate the reader's imagination. Serials, which calculate the location of a cut, deliberately prolong the tension. "The result is that we try to imagine how the story will unfold, and in this way we heighten our own participation in the course of events." Iser, p. 191. The nature of spiritual direction narratives creates this kind of suspension because directees are narrating stories which have not yet

been brought to a conclusion. The imaginative participation of the director in the directee's stories can tempt a director to satisfy his or her curiosity about an unresolved plotline. This curiosity could interfere with the directee's freedom to tell the story he or she needs to narrate after the time lapse.

[18] Jelinek, p. 17.

[19] Suzanne Juhasz, "Towards a Theory of Form in Feminist Autobiography"; Kate Millett's *Flying* and *Sita;* Maxine Hong Kingston's "The Woman Warrior," in *Women's Autobiography,* ed. Jelinek, p. 223.

[20] Paul Janowiak offered me this lively description of the way he experienced the difference between men's and women's narratives:

> Paul: There is more control in men's stories, whereas a woman will tend to go off into the clear blue yonder, like talking about a flower. A man would be more reticent to talk that way. Men don't refer to themselves in organic images that often. Women's stories tend to be more fused with nature images and less controlled.
>
> Interviewer: Do they seem to you to be more rambling, less coherent?
>
> Paul: No, it's just that they will interject feelings into the experience more. I think men tend to report the experience more as it happened. Men tend to report actions. He said this, and then I said that. He did this and I did that, etc.
>
> Interviewer: When they tell you what happened, do they tend to use metaphors?

Paul: What comes to mind is that it is more common for me to hear women say: it was as if I were a flower and I was opening up. I don't remember men using that kind of imagery as often as women. A man would be more likely to say, "I guess I'm becoming more mature" as opposed to "I feel myself kind of opening up." Interview with Paul Janowiak, Berkeley, California, 14 December 1984.

[21] What seemed to be happening to me in these conversations was the opportunity to name my own reality and trust my experience. It marked the awakening of my own feminist consciousness as I experienced the freedom to tell myself (construct my unique identity) and tell my sacred stories. See Carol Christ on the importance of such storytelling for women, *Diving Deep and Surfacing* (Boston: Beacon, 1980), p. 1.

[22] This phrase comes from a poem by Emily Dickinson in which she says: "Tell all the Truth but tell it slant—Success in Circuit lies." Emily Dickinson, Poem #427 (1129), *Final Harvest,* ed. Thomas H. Johnson (Boston: Little, Brown, and Company), p. 248.

[23] Karl Rahner, *Foundations,* pp. 60–67.

[24] Denis Edwards, *Human Experience,* p. 28.

[25] John Shea, *Stories of God* (Chicago: Thomas More, 1978), pp. 24–25.

[26] William J. Bausch in *Storytelling: Imagination and Faith* (Mystic, Connecticut: Twenty-Third Publications, 1984) collects a large number of such stories from a variety of sources.

[27] Edwards, p. 27.

[28] Henri Nouwen, *Reaching Out* (Garden City, New York: Doubleday, 1975).

[29] John Shea, *Stories of Faith* (Chicago: Thomas More, 1980), p. 15.

[30] According to Joseph Powers, "Since life-stories are human stories, they are stories of a truth not yet in complete possession, but a truth to be found in fidelity to the search for the meaning of life in the face of the death which confronts every human." "The Art of Believing," *Theological Studies* 39 (December 1978):664.

[31] Shea, *Stories of Faith,* p. 29.

[32] Ibid., pp. 29, 32–33.

[33] Interview with James and Carmen Neafsey, Berkeley, California, 28 February 1985, and interview with Francis Houdek, Berkeley, California, 18 January 1985. These three directors were particularly conscious of the change in narrational style. Prof. Houdek also pointed out that by contrast a facile use of religious jargon to describe God experience might indicate the directee was using "God-talk" to evade or control an encounter with mystery.

Chapter Seven

[1] This truth is neither the director's nor the directee's but "transcends the subjective opinions of the partners." Hans-Georg Gadamer, *Truth and Method,* p. 331.

[2] Ibid., p. 321.

[3] Ibid., pp. 321–22.

[4] Ibid., p. 322.

[5] Ibid., p. 323. In this case according to Gadamer, the director's "own self-awareness consists precisely in his withdrawing from the dialectic of this reciprocity, in his reflecting himself out of his relation to the other and so becoming

unreachable by him. By understanding the other, by claiming to know him, one takes from him all justification of his own claims. The dialectic of charitable or welfare work in particular operates in this way, penetrating all relationships between men as a reflective form of the effort to dominate. The claim to understand the other person in advance performs the function of keeping the claim of the other person at a distance."

[6] Ibid., p. 324.

[7] Interview with Paul Janowiak. Berkeley, California, 14 December 1984. Jim Neafsey described something similar when he and Carmen were reflecting on their doing spiritual direction as a couple. "The . . . things I feel, I know that Carmen has felt this too, is the experience of God during that hour with a person. It is kind of like a miniconversion during our day, calling us to be present to God. This is something we have seen together, especially as a couple. We are together more than we would ordinarily be, and in a more peaceful place, a place where we are mutually participating in God's presence." Interview with James and Carmen Neafsey, 28 February 1985.

[8] John Shea, *Stories of Faith,* pp. 24–25.

[9] Wolfgang Iser, *The Act of Reading,* p. 35.

[10] Roy Schafer, *The Analytic Attitude,* p. 219.